ARKANSAS

ARKANSAS

A People and Their Reputation

David M. Tucker

MEMPHIS STATE UNIVERSITY PRESS

Copyright © 1985 by Memphis State University Press

All rights reserved. No part of this book may be reproduced or utilized in any form or by any means, electronic or mechanical, including photocopying and recording, without permission from the publisher, except by a reviewer who may quote brief passages in a review.

Manufactured in the United States of America

International Standard Book Number 0-87870-211-3

Library of Congress Cataloging in Publication Data

Tucker, David M., 1937-
  Arkansas : a people and their reputation.

  Bibliography: p.
  Includes index.
  1. Arkansas—History   I. Title.
F411.T83 1985   976.7   85-15511
ISBN 0-87870-211-3

Contents

Preface

In the libraries of the nation the shelves devoted to the history of Arkansas are fewer than those given to books of other states. The impoverishment of local writing has been so severe that no historian has published a general survey for the reading public in more than a generation. We have only the narratives of a poet and a journalist—John Gould Fletcher's *Arkansas* (Chapel Hill, 1947) and Harry S. Ashmore's *Arkansas* (New York, 1979).

A fresh synthesis of the Arkansas past should be informed by the academic writing of the past generation and some understanding of the new social history. The core of the story must shift away from governors and politicians to the people—the society and culture—while preserving the traditional narrative form. To be sure, some politicians, such as Orval Faubus and Jeff Davis, remain too important to ignore, but so are religion, economics, and race.

Our state, the only one in America to fall into bankruptcy three times, and always near the bottom in all the important statistics, has long suffered an image problem. Recent media treatment of Arkansas, however, has been so glamorous that an appropriate title for that history might be "The Cinderella State." Arkansas has long truggled against her own dark and misguided family members: her story is one of conflict with her own worst enemy—Arkansans. Arkansas history is the struggle of frontier against civilization, planters versus common people, Jeff Davis against progress, and whites against blacks. Only in the 1970s did Arkansans finally gain confidence that they had been delivered from themselves. While the Cinderella metaphor conveys much truth, somber historians argue that fairy tales never come true in real life, states never escape their history, and such a title sounds too much like a Chamber of Commerce brochure.

A second criticism of the Cinderella metaphor comes from

chauvinistic southerners who still view the North as the enemy and insist that Cinderella's stepmother and the stepsisters be identified as Yankee oppressors. "This book," an angry critic said, "would be of use to those professional South-haters who continue to use the South as a whipping boy for all of the nation's ills, and who thus draw attention away from the very real evils and difficulties that remain undiagnosed while the nation's witch-doctors hunt for ills beyond their own back yard." Many Arkansans have long blamed outsiders for their problems, but such paranoia is now happily disappearing. To avoid inciting those remaining defensive residents, as well as dour historians, I dropped preliminary plans to title my work "The Cinderella State."

This spare interpretative narrative seeks to tell the story of how modern Arkansas emerged. Native American Indians, as well as the French, have been excluded because they played no significant role in that story, which begins with the Scotch-Irish and the African settlement of the new country. It continues with the evangelical Christians who civilized, the planters who exploited, and the citizens who divided over freedom for slaves. The black struggle for a place in Arkansas is told along with the poverty politics of the distressed cotton farmers, the booster politics of the economic developers, and the exodus of almost a million Arkansans. Recent economic and social changes which moved the state from the days of Dixie to those of the Sunbelt complete the story.

Women are largely missing from the narrative. In a rural, traditional society, women rarely played public roles. To be sure, in 1932, Hattie Caraway became the first woman elected to the United States Senate, but her election had little to do with feminism. A man, Huey P. Long, invaded the state with a loud speaking motor caravan, Louisiana state employees, and two tons of campaign literature to win a victory for the quiet widow of the late Senator Caraway, but even more a victory for Long's own Great Depression campaign against Wall Street and great American fortunes. The public record of Arkansas women has been restricted and their private and community lives so little studied that their history remains yet to be written.

My native point of view comes from Unionist-Republican ancestors in the hill country. I have been both a resident and an outside observer. The first half of my life was lived entirely in Arkansas and the second two decades outside the state. As a student and a corporal in the Arkansas National Guard during the Faubusite rebellion of 1957 I took a college course in "Arkansas" which was clearly the worst of my undergraduate history—anecdotal and lacking in either relevance or intellectual merit. Only after two decades in social, black, and urban history did I regain an interest in Arkansas and offer this essay as my contribution towards providing a more adequate instruction in local history.

Acknowledgements

Arkansas: A People and their Reputation benefited from critical readings by fellow historians—S. Charles Bolton, John Ferguson, Jim Lester, William S. Powell, George H. Thompson, and Bill Worthen. Especially influential were the searching criticisms of Willard B. Gatewood, Jr., who objected to my Cinderella optimism about Arkansas. Surely the dash of realism insisted on by my fellow scholars projects a historical understanding more consistent with the lessons of the Arkansas past.

I would also like to thank the following organizations for use of photographs from their archives:

Arkansas Department of Parks and Tourism: The State Capitol, Little Rock (on the cover).

In the photo insert, in order: Arkansas Department of Parks and Tourism: The Old State House, Little Rock.

Arkansas History Commission: Cadron Settlement, *above and* Cotton Boat at Batesville, *below;* The Brooks-Baxter War, *above and* Old Offices of the *Arkansas Gazette, below;* Logging in the Mt. Pine area c. 1920, *above and* Log raft at Newport, Jackson Couty, *below.*

Library of Congress: Split log fence from the hill country in August 1936 by Dorothea Lange, *above and* Street Life in Clarksville during August 1935 by Arthur Rothstein, *below;* Sharecroppers on the Wilson Plantation in Mississippi County during August 1935 by Arthur Rothstein, *above and* Saturday afternoon on a Delta plantation in August 1938 by Dorothea Lange; Cultivating cotton with mule teams at Lake Dick in June 1938 by Dorothea Lange, *above.*

Arkansas Department of Parks and Tourism: Greers Ferry Dam, *below;* Bear Creek lake in St. Francis National Forest.

To my parents, Hallene and M.C. Tucker,
who introduced me to history.

ARKANSAS

Beaver Lake

Bull Shoals Lake

Lake Norfolk

OZARK

Fayetteville

MOUNTAINS

White R.

Black R.

ARKANSAS

Lake Dardanelle

Greer's Ferry Lake

CROWLEY'S RIDGE

St. Francis R.

Fort Smith

VALLEY

Searcy

West Memphis

OUACHITA

Petit Jean R.

LOWLANDS

Blue Mountain Lake

La Fave R.

Lake Conway

Lake Nimrod

MTS.

Lake Ouachita

Little Rock

Helena

Lake Hamilton

Hot Springs

Lake Catherine

GRAND

PRAIRIE

La Grue Bayou

Lake Greeson

Pine Bluff

Arkansas R.

White R.

ARKANSAS

Arkadelphia

Little Missouri R.

Millwood Lake

Red R.

Fulton

Ouachita R.

DELTA

0 10 20 30 40 50
Miles

SOUTHERN

Texarkana

LOWLANDS

MSU Cartographic Services Laboratory

1

The New Country

The state of Arkansas grew as one branch of the great human migration which moved west after the American Revolution. The land-hungry pioneers had pushed down the long Appalachian valley, where Interstate 81 now runs, from Pennsylvania to North Carolina, crossing over into South Carolina or the new territories of Alabama, Tennessee, and Kentucky. Leading the migration of the backcountry pioneers were hunters who moved far in advance of farming settlements, living off the great forest while hunting deer, bear, and buffalo or trapping beaver and otter. Even before Americans had won their war of independence, Kentucky hunters were exploring the new country beyond the Mississippi River. And within a single generation after the Revolution, the United States government had purchased the French claim to the Mississippi valley and the first wave of settlers arrived in Arkansas.

The human migration blended an American mix of Scotch-Irish, English, and German peoples. The Scotch-Irish who dominated the southern migration were descendants of proud but primitive lowland Scots who, after hardening by a meager existence in a barren country, took advantage of the British invitation of 1610 to colonize northern Ireland and dispossess Irish Catholics of their

1

land. These Presbyterian Scots pioneered in northern Ireland, conquering the forest and fighting back the wolves and the Irish. A hundred years later Scots from northern Ireland moved on to America where they bypassed the settled eastern communities and moved out to the Pennsylvania frontier, settling on Indian lands in the Great Valley of the Appalachians. They were regarded by older settlers as a restless, impetuous people who lacked the steadiness or culture of English and Germans. Their ethnic genes, however, were surely not inferior since professors in the Scottish universities had dominated the intellectual life of the British enlightenment. And the Scotch-Irish who settled down in America demonstrated a commitment to schools and education equal to that of the older English communities; but those who pushed on south, down the valley into the Carolina backcountry, continued to offer examples of crude and slovenly frontier life-styles ridiculed by observers from the civilized eastern communities.[1]

The Scotch-Irish composed perhaps one-seventh of the white population at the time of the American Revolution. In the back-country, however, and in the move west to the new lands they were a majority. They were no longer predominately Scotch-Irish in out-look; after two generations they had ceased to think of themselves as a minority group. They had become Americans, just as likely to marry sons and daughters of English or German neighbors as to become Baptists or Methodists. Some men even married native American Indian women. Cherokee and Choctaw traits were thus united with European blood in forming the frontier people. The settlers who moved across the Appalachians, down the Cumberland and the Tennessee rivers, and across the Mississippi to new country were Americans blended in a frontier environment which thought the distinctions of hunter, settler, and planter more important than ethnic background.

For a clear window on the first wave of Arkansas settlement one can read the description of Russell Benedict who, as a boy in 1818, moved with his family across the wilderness. The Benedicts avoided the eastern swamps and sunken lands created by the great earthquake of 1811 by entering the new country from Missouri. As the family moved across the wilderness with a wagon, following an old Indian trail where U.S. 67 would later run, they saw few whites and those were hunters who existed on wild game and lived without planting a hill of corn or even a garden patch. According to Benedict, none of the families then living on the Arkansas River at Cadron Creek had sufficient culture to plant a vegetable garden or wear anything but deerskin, moccasins, and coonskin caps. The hunters were devoid of either education or religion, resisting all civilization by moving on west at the first sight of new settlers.[2]

Benedict's recollection documents the settler's disapproval of the hunter life-style but it surely exaggerates in implying that the Benedicts were the first settlers to move among the hunters. Four years earlier, a traveling Methodist preacher found other farmers when he crossed the Arkansas wilderness from southeast Missouri to the Texas border. The Reverend William Stevenson observed a great many small settlements, from five to twenty miles apart, along the rivers and streams. These communities, according to Stevenson, were inhabited by "industrious people, but among them many hunters."[3] Stevenson agreed that only settlers were industrious people; the hunters represented an uncivilized and unchristian lifestyle.

While hunters rarely farmed or bought land, they did operate within the market system of trade to acquire rifles, powder, lead, knives, horseshoes, iron pots, and blankets. In addition to harvesting furs and skins, hunters also transported wild honey to the old French trading village of Arkansas Post and to Jacob Barkman's settlement on the Ouachita. English colonists had brought over the European honeybee which escaped from captivity and multiplied, making honey from wild flowers and storing it in hollow trees; they advanced ahead of Americans into the wilderness. Hunters were also herdsmen with hogs and cattle grazing wild upon the public land. Livestock provided food and could also be a cash crop sold to new settlers, to Arkansas Post, or in New Orleans. Rivers were the commercial arteries where flatboats, constructed of logs to the dimensions of twelve by forty feet, floated frontier products down the Arkansas rivers and the Mississippi to New Orleans.[4]

The industrious Benedict family represented not the hunters or the traders but the wave of agricultural settlers who brought seeds to plant and the ambition to level the great forest. Trees and shade were incompatible with crops; they stole the sunshine, moisture, and soil nutriments. Trees harbored enemies who would ravage growing crops—raccoons, squirrels, and jaybirds. And settlers had also learned that trees could harbor hostile Indians. Although Arkansas Indians were peaceful, except for the Osage, settlers remembered the Carolina and Kentucky Indian wars and firmly wished to cut every tree in sight and let the sunshine in.

To clear the land, to construct fencing and housing, the settler brought the American axe—the most important tool in the new country. After selecting a good spot of land convenient to some spring or creek, the settler needed about forty tall, straight trees for a log cabin. He felled the trees with his single-bitted axe, cut the trunks into fifteen and twenty-foot lengths, and dragged them to the housing site with the assistance of a pair of oxen. Perhaps the settler even squared the logs with the aid of a broadaxe and smoothed the floor timbers with a hoe-shaped axe called an adze, and surely he split the roofing boards with a frow. Then he invited his neighbors to a house raising.[5]

An expert axeman stood at each cabin corner to cut the notches while the other men and boys carried and raised the logs. The cabin rose with amazing speed, the entrance for a door and the fireplace was chopped or sawed out and by the end of the day only the roofing or fireplace construction remained for the owner to finish by himself. To be sure, the finishing touches, the door, shelves, chinking the cracks with clay, and constructing wooden furniture might be postponed for some time.

Before planting the Indian garden seeds—corn, pumpkins, and beans—the settler cleared a small field. Some of the largest and straightest oaks were cut and split by wedges into fence rails. These zig-zag fences—six to ten rails high—encircled the field and protected the crops from the hogs, cattle, and deer that ran loose. Once the settler split enough rails to encircle his field, he never cut down all the other trees but followed the land-clearing practice of American Indians. He ruined the huge giants easily by chopping a circle of bark around each trunk and left the killed tree standing. The underbrush he uprooted with a heavy grubbing hoe, the mattock, and piled it for burning. The settler then plowed among the stumps and the deadened trees of the ruined forest, planting perhaps ten acres of Indian corn, the principal pioneer food. Limbs from the dead trees began falling on the crop within a year or two, the trunks toppled over in three or four years. The new ground for corn and another fifteen-acre patch for cotton, the market crop, required an annual clean-up, chopping, piling, and burning, until even the tree stumps finally rotted after six to ten years.

Frequently the settler had cleared his field of stumps before he ever gained a government title to the farm. Government surveyors lagged behind the first wave of enterprising settlers, surveying only half the land in Arkansas by 1840. But even ten years later, when purchase was possible, eighty-six percent of settlers in the western county of Van Buren remained squatters on government land. Many early pioneers clearly preferred to wait, to live tax-free on public land, and then to sell their improvements and preemption rights to a more prosperous emigrant. The western politicians had protected the interests of these squatters by legislating preemption laws which permitted original settlers to buy their land at the minimum price of $1.25 an acre. So the same impulse which had originally moved the early pioneer to follow the setting sun in search of new land often moved him again and again.[6]

Farmers and hunters never monopolized the pioneering spirit. Traders and merchants had preceded farmers to the new land where the old French town—Arkansas Post—had existed for more than a hundred years as a military outpost and an Indian trading center. Arkansas Post attracted enterprising Americans from the North who joined the more than thirty families living there. The ambitious William Woodruff, who founded the first newspaper in the territory, the *Arkansas Gazette,* came to make his fortune, but quickly moved on to Little Rock in 1821 when the politicians shifted the territorial capital away from the mosquito-infested swamps up the river to higher ground across from Big Rock. Little Rock became the Arkansas center for enterprise, trade, and politics.[7]

The process of emigration rapidly gained speed after Arkansas became an organized territory, in 1819, with the population more than doubling in every decade. As the federal government moved out all Indian tribes—Choctaws, Osage, Cherokee—by the end of the 1820s, whites poured into Arkansas. Settlers from Tennessee, Alabama, Georgia, and the Carolinas thronged the military road from Memphis. Where census takers found only 14,000 residents in 1820 they counted 435,000 forty years later. And Woodruff's *Gazette* boasted, as early as 1840, that Arkansas had ceased to be a howling wilderness. "Forests have fallen; the red man has disappeared; and the bear and the deer have scarce an abiding place. Ware-houses, steam-boats, and the busy hum of man salute you at our wharves; drays and various other vehicles fill our streets—brick stores stand with the textures and products of every clime."[8]

The *Gazette* surely exaggerated the disappearance of the wilderness since a wild bear devoured a sixteen-year-old youth only a dozen miles from Little Rock in 1852. Packs of hunting hounds were as common as commercial drays in the capital city where grass grew in the dirt streets along with wild Cherokee roses and there were only "a few" brick houses. Yet commerce did flow through the political and trade center built astride the main routes to Texas and to the Indian territory. Federal money fueled the early Arkansas economy as steamboats of supplies were moved up the Arkansas River to Fort Smith and the Indian nations. Government purchases of beef, agricultural equipment, and spinning wheels brought money into the Arkansas economy and provided Little Rock with regular steamboat transportation.[9]

The cotton plantation economy had also moved into Arkansas with the new immigration. While it was true that slavery and a few blacks had existed in Arkansas long before the United States acquired the French claim in 1803, early settlers brought few slaves into the territory. The largest slaveholder in the territory claimed only thirty-three slaves in 1830, but during the next decade slaves came in increasing numbers, boosting their percentage of the population from eleven percent in 1820 to twenty percent in 1840. By the fall of 1834 the *Arkansas Gazette* reported large droves of slaves and masters daily passing through Little Rock on their way to the Red River valley where government land was selling at auction for amazing prices as high as $20 an acre. The rich land attracted prosperous Scotch-Irish families from as far away as North Carolina. Hempstead, the Red River county on the Texas border, temporarily became the leading slave county but later dropped behind delta counties along the Arkansas and Mississippi rivers. By 1860 three-fourths of the 111,259 slaves lived in the thirty lowland counties where plantations generally included two to six black families—ten to thirty individuals on the average. Only sixty-six plantations owned more than a hundred slaves.[10]

The emerging cotton plantations stood on the edge of the forest. Log cabins and partially cleared fields were more typical than whitewashed mansions and clean fields. Plantation blacks remembered sharing much of the pioneering experience. Dock Wilborn, as a twelve-year-old slave, moved with the four Wilborn brothers of Alabama and their hundred slaves to wild undeveloped land in Phillips County in 1855. Wilborn later recalled with pride that in this wilderness they had built cabins, deadened the timber, and planted a cotton crop. In a wild country where little of the land was touched by axe or plow in 1860, blacks as well as whites lived in log cabins, ate bear meat, and practiced the pioneer arts.[11]

Much of Arkansas still appeared to be a new country in 1860. The main dirt road from Memphis remained impassable through the east Arkansas swamps for much of the year. Only two million out of the state's thirty-three million acres were "improved." Arkansas remained predominately a forest without cities (Little Rock counted only 3,727 people), without canals, banks, or railroads, although a rail connection with Memphis was under construction. The architecture outside Little Rock remained predominately log cabin, although no longer of the single room variety. The new double-pen log house offered two rooms connected by a hallway. Separate rooms helped to make the hot summers more bearable: cooking in the open kitchen fireplace only heated one room, leaving the other and the breezy hall at normal summer heat. [12] Glass windows no longer created astonishment but, of course, window screening remained a luxury for the future, which left little escape from mosquitoes and fever except by avoiding the rich lowlands for the poorer hill country.

Arkansas neared the end of her frontier experience long before the pioneer architecture disappeared. As Malcolm Rohrbough has explained, the end of the frontier came first in a man's heart when he realized that the land had become occupied, the county court established, taxes collected, the common law accepted, schools and churches established. By 1860 the 435,450 residents had occupied much of the better land, leaving only the swampy lowlands cursed by overflows and deadly fevers, and the poor lands of the Ozark and Ouachita mountains. In the isolated Buffalo River valley settlement took longer, and a squatter might live beyond 1900 without filing for a title to his homestead. But these mountain pockets of pioneer life surely lacked the high expectations shared by the first settlers who had moved into Arkansas when it had been a new land of infinite possibilities.[13]

2

Redeeming the People

Frontier Arkansas suffered violence, crime, and cultural depriva-
tion. Greedy, hot-tempered men fleeing the restrictions and pen-
alties of civilized society moved to the new territory. The murderer,
horse-thief, or debtor who escaped the reach of the sheriff found
freedom to begin anew on the frontier. And if these social misfits
or men of violent temper again committed murder in the new land
they were unlikely to be punished for their crime. So permissive
were the social standards of Arkansas that even the speaker of the
first state House of Representatives could silence a critic on the
floor of the legislature with a Bowie knife and go free to be elected
again to represent Arkansans.

John Wilson, the knife-wielding speaker, who represented the
Red River counties of Hempstead and Clark for seventeen years
during territorial days, also became president of the new Real Estate Bank. When an opponent of the bank, Representative Joseph
J. Anthony, made a quip about the bank president, Wilson ordered
him to sit down. When Anthony refused, Wilson drew his knife,
saying, "Then, I will make you." Anthony, a veteran of the War of
1812 and Andrew Jackson's war on the Creeks, drew his own knife
in self-defense against the advancing Speaker. The two met across

9

an upraised chair and Anthony drew first blood by striking across the chair, cutting Wilson on the left arm. Anthony's second blow missed, his wrist struck the chair, and his knife clattered to the floor. The weaponless Anthony retreated, but Wilson pursued, raised Anthony's chair with his left arm and deliberately thrust his knife into his critic's heart. Although Anthony died immediately on the floor of the Arkansas House of Representatives, Speaker Wilson was not arrested until a relative of the deceased demanded a warrant for the arrest three days later. At the murder trial, the jury brought a verdict of "excusable homicide," freeing Wilson to treat the jury members with a night of drinking, dancing, and trumpeting. The Arkansas House had expressed disapproval of Wilson's parliamentary leadership by expelling him, but he was reelected to the legislature in 1840, before finally moving on to Texas.[1]

The Wilson murder certainly helped to confirm the name of "Arkansas" as a synonym of outlawry and violence. Pictured as a howling wilderness populated by Bowie-knife men, blood-thirsty fighters, and refugees from law and order, Arkansas offered a splendid example to document the northern abolitionist charge that slavery spread a poison producing regular atrocities on whites as well as blacks. The Arkansas "toothpick," the first Bowie blade, had been hammered out by a Hempstead County blacksmith. Statesmen of Arkansas, even judges and politicians, had killed each other in deadly duels. While it was true that other southern states also suffered from personal violence, only Arkansas had been shamed by a Speaker of the House who killed with a knife in a flash of anger at a slighting remark.[2]

Concern for the state reputation did trouble those Arkansans who feared that bad publicity would depress emigration, land speculation, and commerce. The *Arkansas Gazette* even began a policy of ignoring local murder and violence in hope of improving the state reputation, elevating the moral standards, and promoting increased emigration to Arkansas. Settlers, who wanted eastern relatives to join them, defended the character of their neighbors. "You have made a great mistake as to our inhabitants," John Meek wrote his South Carolina son-in-law, "the people composing our community are the enterprising citizens of Europe and America . . . the people are a church-going people and they greatly pride themselves in being orderly when at church."³

Arkansas boosters surely exaggerated the early triumph of decency but much evidence exists to confirm that the cruder days of frontier violence had already passed when the horrible 1837 House of Representatives murder occurred. In fact, Speaker Wilson feared to be tried by a Little Rock jury and moved his case to the more primitive Saline County courts. Little Rock had reformed its moral climate, according to one observer, after the first regular minister of the gospel began preaching to the town of forty-six log cabins, eight frame, and six brick buildings. This observer, a Boston-born printer for the *Arkansas Gazette*, described Little Rock in 1827 as inhabited by the human dregs of the southwest, "a more drunken good-for-nothing set of fellows never got together." "The Secretary of the Territory and the Judges of the Supreme Court drink whiskey out of the same cup with the lowest vagabond, and roll together in the same gutter. There has been more than a dozen murders here. The greatest drunkards fill the most responsible offices." The following year, after Presbyterian minister James Moore arrived from Princeton Theological Seminary, the printer observed a striking improvement.

> There has been a great change in this place within a few weeks. We have had a minister of the gospel preaching here for some time. His labors are likely to be crowned with success. The women of the community were the first to interest themselves in religion, and several joined the Presbyterian and Baptist churches. Lately, the young men have been affected, and many that a few weeks since were a pest to society are now an ornament to it. Instead of drinking and gambling at the taverns, they are now reading the Bible and conversing with the preacher.

And two years later, in 1830, printer Hiram Whittington recorded continued progress in morality despite his own lack of religious faith.

> Since we have had preaching here—about two years—everything has changed. The pistol and the dirk have been laid aside. The people, instead of racing horses and fighting chickens on Sunday, attend public worship. The children are kept clean. During the week they are sent to school and to Sunday School on the Sabbath. . . . There is hardly a child in the place but what

attends very regularly. It is conducted about three hours every Sunday. All the ladies attend as teachers, even the wife of the governor, although she is 70 years of age, and she is a regular teacher in the Sunday School. Besides the wives of our Superior Court Judges, even the young ladies, although they are not religious, attend as teachers. If you could have seen Little Rock four years ago and see it now, you would never say that religion was all a bugbear and preachers mere drones in society.[4]

As adventurers and refugees from justice continued to pour into Little Rock, multiplying its population to 1500 within a decade, religion failed to socialize all the new migrants. Later observers reported concealed pistols and Bowie knives as well as two-thirds of the inhabitants skipping Sunday worship services. No historian could say that preachers made Little Rock a city of God, but certainly religion appears to have been the major force in reducing violence and in establishing social order not only in Little Rock but in the whole of Arkansas as well, where the Christian denominations were actively evangelizing the state.

The religion of the frontier was neither the old established state churches of colonial America—Anglican and Congregational—nor the French Catholic Church—but instead the new dissenter sects which had been the smallest religious groups at the time of the American Revolution. Methodists and Baptists, whose small numbers placed them at the bottom of American membership lists in 1775, evangelized their way to the top by 1860. In Arkansas, Methodists won 57.3 percent of the state's church members and the Baptists followed with 23.9 percent. The Presbyterian faith, which had been the Scotch-Irish religion, retained few members because of its reluctance to evangelize the West. The Presbyterian Church generally waited for laymen to form a congregation and call a minister rather than sending out evangelizing preachers to build new religious communities. Presbyterians also maintained educational requirements for the ministry, thus restricting the supply of ministers and losing many Scotch-Irish to the more popular Methodists and Baptists. A western Presbyterian splinter group, the Cumberland Presbyterians, dropped the educational requirement for ministers and reached the frontier ahead of the parent church; one of its members, John Carnahan, was the first Protestant preacher to move to Arkansas, in 1811. But the two Presbyterian churches together recruited only 11.8 percent of Arkansas church members in 1860.[5]

Arkansas Methodism began with William Stevenson, a Scot born on the Carolina frontier in 1768. He had moved west to teach school in East Tennessee and then to farm on the Cumberland River above Nashville during the Great Revival of 1800. Stevenson never experienced the emotional trances or jerks that characterized this revival but in private prayer he did experience a conversion and then joined the Methodist church. Within a couple of years the industrious Stevenson became a licensed local preacher in Tennessee. When he moved west to the cheaper lands of Missouri in 1809 with neighbors and relatives, Stevenson continued as a farmer and local exhorter, preaching to his neighbors and to camp meetings.[6]

In the fall of 1814 Stevenson's brother, who had emigrated to the Red River country of southwest Arkansas, visited Missouri and persuaded William to go back with him and take Methodism to Arkansas. The Stevenson brothers rode horseback across 200 miles of wilderness, where settlements existed only on the rivers, and established a few small Methodist societies. The next year William Stevenson became a full-time circuit rider, appointed by the Missouri Methodist Conference. He sold his Missouri farm and moved with more than half of his local congregation in a wagon train to Mound Prairie on the Red River where the first Methodist church building in Arkansas would be erected.

The Methodist circuit rider created congregations in every settlement and recruited farmers to assist in nurturing the new Methodist societies. The local unpaid preachers far outnumbered the salaried circuit riders and contributed much to the growth of Methodism, holding regular Sunday worship services and weekly class meetings in the many isolated communities of Arkansas. An amusing frontier story is told of a local preacher, Eli Lindsey, who stopped his sermon when the hunting dogs left outside began pursuit of a bear. "The service is adjourned in order that the men may kill that bear," the farmer-preacher declared. And after the successful hunt, Lindsey renewed his sermon, "thanking God for men who knew how to shoot and for women who knew how to pray." Lindsey was probably too secular to have been a good Methodist preacher; he added only three new members and seems to have served only an 1816 appointment.

The organization of circuit riders and local preachers helped Arkansas Methodism more than double the membership of its nearest rival—the Baptists. Methodism's avoidance of theological controversy surely helped, too. Their preachers were little interested in debate over doctrine—they could baptise either by immersion or sprinkling—and they spent little time ferreting out theological error. Saving souls and reforming the nation with a religion of the heart was the important mission for Methodists. They demanded only a personal conversion experience and a moral life. The Methodists democratically allowed every man to save himself by good works despite any error he might embrace in theology. Within a decade the Arkansas Methodist recruited 2500 members, one-fifth of whom were black. And the state membership continued to more than double in every following decade.

The Baptists rejected centralized authority with its paid circuit riders and were therefore less successful in frontier evangelizing. Established Baptist congregations, however, did form associations to maintain orthodoxy and send out occasional itinerants. In 1817 the Missouri Bethel Baptist Association sent the Reverend James Phillip Edwards to preach in Arkansas and to organize the Salem Baptist Church at Fourche de Thomas. Baptist congregations also developed with little or no assistance from other associations. When a Kentucky silversmith, Silas T. Toncray, moved to the new town of Little Rock in 1824 no church of any denomination existed. Toncray and a dozen Baptists built a log church and he served as pastor. Toncray's church did request that the eastern Baptist Home Mission Society make Arkansas a field for organizing. During the next decade the society supported missionaries for Arkansas, first hiring the Reverend David Orr from Missouri in 1832.[7]

Missionaries aroused opposition from some Baptists who resented the more educated missionary ministers. Missionaries were declared unscriptural. Only God, operating through a congregation, the critics said, could call a minister. The institutions of man, the society boards, conventions, and theological schools, they charged, threatened to begin a church hierarchy unauthorized by the Bible. These antimissionaries, Hard Shells as they were called, took a predestinarian position that God would save the elect without the interference of man and his institutions. Hard Shells also insisted on retaining the custom of Christian touching as one of the ordinances of the Bible—the right hand of fellowship, the kiss of charity and the washing of feet. Perhaps one-fourth of the eighty Baptist churches and the 2655 members in 1848 were antimissionary. But otherwise Baptist beliefs were essentially the same. All agreed that preachers should be unsalaried farmers or businessmen who had experienced a call to preach and been licensed by a congregation after a trial sermon. Members agreed to watch over each other in brotherly tenderness to fulfill the law of Christ. Monthly business sessions, controlled by majority vote, heard charges of public offenses and decided upon censure or exclusion from the church. Among ardent believers, fearful of social stigma and worried about the destiny of their eternal souls, to be expelled was a terrible thing.[8]

The weekly church discipline imposed on the members has largely been forgotten by historians who focus on the emotionalism and lack of book learning among the frontier clergy of the Baptists and Methodists. Weekly discipline imposed by frontier congregations persisted long after revivals were over. Evangelical Christianity sought not only individual conversion experiences but also to replace the disorder of the world with the order of a Christian society. Converted sinners must not be permitted to lapse back into worldly behavior. Each denomination, especially Baptists, had a group discipline spelling out decent standards for Christian life and charging each congregation to work as a watch committee to control the spiritual growth and behavior of its members. Converts were never free individuals to do as they pleased. The 1842 minutes of the Washington Association of Baptists in northwest Arkansas reported 120 baptised, 34 dismissed, 7 excluded, and 11 restored. Almost eight percent of the fellowship had been dismissed or excluded since the previous association meeting. The Baptists and other denominations clearly prohibited their members from engaging in murder, dueling, fighting, drunkenness, gambling, swearing, card playing, dancing, gossiping, and self-indulgence. Congregations were especially concerned with sin which disrupted the family—fornication, adultery, and marital squabbles. Each congregation conducted hearings and trials of members accused of breaching church discipline. Offending members were censured, placed on probation, or expelled by congregations seeking to uphold moral standards.[9]

It would be a failure to understand frontier Arkansas if we assume the churches exaggerated the evils of alcohol. Within that culture, drinking often led to violence and degradation. In *Early Days in Arkansas,* William F. Pope speaks of men who came to a tragic end, became "hard drinkers," quarrelsome, and died in a knife fight. The rival Tutt-Everett families of the lethal Marion County war were "hard drinkers" of "fighting whiskey." The mix of alcohol and violent people led to social madness, threatening women and children with the likelihood of becoming widows and orphans. The prohibition efforts of the churches were surely steps toward establishing social order.[10]

Women and religion worked together in Arkansas much as had frontiersmen and violence. New country always attracted an overwhelming preponderance of males for the adventures of exploring, hunting, and pioneering. The masculine society gambled, drank, and fought until women arrived to insist on the feminine rights of security and family stability. Religion reflected the world of women, who were always more attracted to congregation meetings than were men. Churches established a public life for women, allowing them to leave the home for outside fellowship as well as a cooperative effort to bring controls over the unruly masculine society. While women were barred from preaching, they could testify of their conversion and work with others in the congregation discipline committee to establish a caring community. Religion and women joined together in converting Arkansas from a frontier into a civilized community.

Religion also improved the treatment of black Arkansans. Despite the testimony of a Maryland black that religion worsened his condition because his converted master then justified whippings by quoting Scripture: "He that knoweth his master's will, and doeth it not, shall be beaten with many stripes," there is much evidence that evangelical Christianity elevated the status of blacks across the American South. Because blacks also experienced emotional conversions, the most important requirement of evangelical religion, blacks were elevated to a common level—saved brothers in Christ. Whites eagerly invited blacks to participate in their services as church members.

Arkansas Baptist congregations actively recruited blacks as members and brothers. The congregation minutes did not always identify a brother by race. The minutes of the Point Remove Congregation, for example, simply record: "Opend a door for the reception of members & Recd Brother Thomas Lemly by Experiance" when black Lemly joined the church. Blacks also led the singing, conducted prayer service, and preached. The Reverend Tom Clements's popularity brought him more than a hundred white funerals to preach. White Baptists believed their Christian duty required bringing the Gospel not only to their own slaves but to all blacks in Arkansas. Through their state convention, after 1848, Baptists sent missionaries to the slaves of unchurched plantation lowlands. [11]

American Methodism had been an abolitionist society when first organized in 1784, and as late as the 1820s the Arkansas presiding elder Jesse Haile forced slaveholders from the ministry, but Methodist hopes of preaching to everyone, including slaveholders, led southern Methodism away from active abolitionism. And in 1844, as the issue of slavery split Methodism sectionally, most of the Arkansas Methodists joined the new Southern Methodist Church. The conscience of the southern church seems to have been expressed through a renewed effort to evangelize blacks, who had always been included in upland congregations, by sending missionaries to the plantation lowland.[12]

Evangelical religion surely taught self-discipline and Christian virtues which planters appreciated as social control, but religion also appealed to blacks because it gave them dignity as human beings. The liberation message of evangelicals, begun among lower class whites of colonial America, also appealed to enslaved blacks. One gained self-esteem from inclusion in a democratic religion which taught that God had no respect for wealth and that Jesus had come to proclaim "liberty to the captives." Because blacks usually shared the same worship services with whites they heard the whole evangelical message. Black religion would thus teach not only good works, and brotherhood with the white man, but also the hope of freedom in this world as well as the next. In their spirituals, blacks sang the Old Testament message that God delivered justice in this world. Over and over the slave songs dwelt upon the spectacle of the Red Sea opening to allow the Hebrew slaves through before sweeping over the mighty armies of the Pharoah. Moses, Joshua, Jonah, and Noah were all delivered in this world. The similarity of these tales to the situation of the slaves was too clear for them not to see it. The songs clearly had a worldly context when blacks sang "O my Lord delivered Daniel, O why not deliver me."Christianity did give blacks hope, courage, and self-esteem as they identified themselves with the Chosen People of the Bible. And the slave preachers who shouted with their congregations but counseled a strategy of patience were not misleading their people. The great judgement day would come with Abraham Lincoln and the Union Armies.[13]

To please the God who gave them self-esteem and a sense of liberation, Arkansas evangelicals, black or white, demanded of themselves and their community the standard of behavior laid out by the Ten Commandments. As communities of believers constructed their rude log churches and enforced godly standards against pride, covetousness, lust, anger, gluttony, envy, and sloth, evil men suffered discomfort and many moved on west where frontier conditions still prevailed.

While the major force for taming frontier Arkansas must be recognized as religion, the business world and the *Arkansas Gazette* played a supporting role. The young Yankee editor, William Woodruff, may have been indifferent to personal religion, yet he spoke for the cultural standards of New York Presbyterianism, condemning dueling, organized gambling, and drunkenness. Woodruff never criticized human slavery, his cultural views became southern, but he stoutly opposed the other crude edges of human behavior, firmly supporting traditional Judeo-Christian ethics taught by the churches.[14]

The newspapers, the churches, and the massive emigration of women from eastern states erased most frontier behavior well before the Civil War. Yet the frontier image of the state remained fixed in the American mind. The mental picture of the state had been so firmly established by amusing literary essays of bears and Bowie knives in the eastern sporting magazine, *Spirit of the Times,* and by the words of the fiddle tune, *The Arkansas Traveler,* that this description would be continued by the next generation of fiction writers—Mark Twain and Opie Read.[15] Frontier Arkansas had been redeemed but the rest of the nation never learned the good news.

3

The Planter Sting

The establishment of state government in Arkansas quickly led to
an economic exploitation of the settlers as the planter class used
state credit to enrich itself and leave the general population with a
debt which ruined state credit and impoverished public services
throughout the nineteenth century. Planters and their banks dam-
aged Arkansas more than any disaster except the Civil War.

The plantation banking disaster grew out of the southern economic expansion of the 1830s. Frenzied real-estate speculation, fi-
nanced by easy credit, fueled a rising land and slave market. As
prices and profits rose like smoke, eager Arkansas planters borrowed money from New Orleans cotton factors and bankers so they
might participate in the feverish capitalistic expansion. The exhil-
aration of acquiring a fortune on borrowed money was limited only
by the shortage of credit. If only Arkansas Territory could be organized into a state then she could create banks and assist her speculative planters in turning the uncleared forest into baronial estates.[1]

Plantation banking offered a scheme for creating easy money
and credit. The system could be built entirely of land mortgages
and the use of state credit. The planter gave a mortgage on his land
in exchange for shares of bank stock. The bank turned these mort-

19

gages over to the state government in exchange for Arkansas bonds which could be sold in the eastern markets to raise the money to lend planters for buying more land and slaves. The plantation bank, which could also print its own money, would be a wonderful wealth machine to enrich not only the planters but Arkansas, too, as it provided the capital required to level the forest, harvest the crops, and market the cotton. Money would flow from the plantations to the towns and to the state. Everyone would gain, or so the planters claimed. Louisiana and Mississippi had plantation banks and why shouldn't Arkansas?

Before a plantation bank could be chartered, the Arkansas Territory should first become a state. Statehood would of course be expensive as the cost of supporting officials and internal improvements were shifted from the federal government to the local citizens. Arkansas would actually have been financially better off to postpone statehood, but her planters could not wait for their bank, they insisted on immediately having statehood and a real estate bank.

The movement for statehood began in 1833 when the Territory of Michigan applied for admission to the Union. Michigan would enter as a free state without human slavery and this, of course threatened to upset the congressional custom of balancing the number of free and slave states. Arkansas planters and representatives claimed that southern patriotism required pushing Arkansas forward as a candidate for statehood to prevent Michigan from tipping the balance of power against slavery. Highland farmers, who had no stake in slavery, were not eager to be taxed for the support of slavery and southern patriotism but the planters advertised statehood as the road to immediate prosperity. Banking, to be sure, was not then made the leading issue in the debate but it was later charged that the planters' desire for banking had been the central reason for pushing Arkansas prematurely into the Union at a time when her population of 52,000 was only half that of Michigan. The planters' desire for banks was certainly strong enough to make a real estate bank the first legislative measure to be enacted after Arkansas became one of the United States in 1836.[2]

The new state of Arkansas emerged firmly in the hands of a small power elite—the planter class—even though that class was yet crude, young, and without great wealth. No Arkansas master possessed a polished mansion or owned more than thirty-three slaves in 1830. In fact, few slaveholders could then even fit the traditional definition of a planter—one who owns more than twenty slaves—but the planter class surely dominated the government through the Conway, Sevier, and Johnson families who held the federally appointed territorial positions. The Arkansas delegate to Congress in 1836, Ambrose H. Sevier, confessed to President Andrew Jackson that perhaps the family held too many of the political plums. Sevier explained to the president:

> Col. Rector at this time is agent for the Creek Indians—His brother Elias Rector, is now Marshal and will expect a reappointment under our state, as soon as it is admitted—James Conway, who is now the incumbent, is Rector's cousin, and is the democratic candidate for governor— Conway is my relation also—I am held up for the Senate in Arkansas, and my father in law Judge Johnson, I desire to be appointed federal Judge—I am thus particular, in order to show you that if Rector is appointed in the place of Conway to the exclusion of Cross, who wants it, the people of Arkansas will consider that there is too much monopoly in the offices of Arkansas by my relatives and intimate friends.[3]

Sevier had been the delegate who introduced the 1833 congressional resolution that Arkansas be permitted to form a constitution preparatory to admission into the Union. And once the Arkansas Real Estate Bank was organized, Sevier, like the other members of his family, pressed for loans to repay outstanding plantation debts, explaining:

> I feel great anxiety to get our banks in operation. I need not disguise to you, that I shall want all the facilities that it can afford me, and that too at as early a date as possible, and for every dollar I want, I had rather have eastern paper, as my debts are at New Orleans, and in this quarter of the world.[4]

The Real Estate Bank had been pushed through against strong opposition from the spokesmen of the highland northwest in both the constitutional convention and the first legislature. The planters bought off some of the opposition by offering to support a second bank for the highlands, a state bank, but still the planter's Real Estate Bank won only a narrow ten-to seven vote approval in the Senate. Upland critics would continue to charge that the bank represented special favoritism as only 184 planters in a dozen lowland counties along the Mississippi, Arkansas, Red, and Ouachita rivers were permitted to be stockholders and to borrow three-fourths of the bank's $2,000,000.[5]

Criticism of the Real Estate Bank led to the murder of Representative Joseph J. Anthony, who had joined other bank opponents in attempting to prevent the Arkansas bonds from being turned over to a private corporation designed "to enrich the few at the expense of the many." Anthony introduced a resolution in the House of Representatives on November 25, 1837, condemning the bank as detrimental to the democratic faith in equal rights and requiring that no action be taken on the bonds until Arkansas voters had expressed their consent in a state referendum. The House, which was controlled by Speaker John Wilson, a planter from the Red River valley who was also bank president, refused to receive the resolution. The following week Anthony made his jesting remark about requiring the signature of the Real Estate Bank president on wolf scalp bounty certificates. The hot-tempered Wilson, stung by the implied accusation, attacked the representative with a knife and murdered him on the floor of the Arkansas House of Representatives.[6]

The killing of Anthony did not help the reputation of the Real Estate Bank with its critics even though John Wilson stepped down from its presidency after his indictment for murder. The bank unfortunately entered business at the wrong peak in the business cycle. It had organized at the height of speculative land prices, but then the economy suffered the New York banking panic of 1837 followed by the 1839 collapse in cotton prices and one of the most severe depressions in American history. Across the nation banks sought to save themselves by calling in and foreclosing mortgages on business houses and plantations, but still these financial institutions failed by the hundreds.

The Real Estate Bank had never been managed by prudent banking policy and therefore, like all other plantation banks, was destined to fail. It began lending out all of its money in December

1838 and within two years it could not pay the interest on the $2,000,000 of Arkansas five-percent bonds which had been sold to eastern investors. When the bond payments fell due, banking officials illegally mortgaged another $500,000 of unsold bonds which became known as the Holford bonds. The real estate officials were less concerned with sound banking practices than with helping their own economic class which needed money to pay prior debts to out-of-state banks and thus avoid bankruptcy. So the officials had recklessly distributed their gold to themselves, printed $854,650 of paper money, and then found themselves unable to raise the gold to pay bond interest due for the year 1841. When the bank defaulted on its interest payment, the state of Arkansas became legally bound to pay the $91,000, more than half the annual state budget, and so Arkansas also defaulted.[7]

What should be done? Bank president and planter Anthony H. Davies, who owed $20,000, explained to eastern creditors that nothing should be done. The Arkansas people were too poor and ignorant to pay. "Ours is a community (at least the mass of it)" he wrote, "that knows nothing of monied or commercial transactions; they do not and cannot understand the moral force of sustaining the public faith; and in the legislature there is neither moral courage nor political honesty enough to do it." If the people and politicians couldn't pay, then why not foreclose on the planters who were refusing to pay their interest? Oh no, President Davies assured, legal action should not be attempted. Foreclosure on mortgages by court action would take two to three years and gain little. "From such a course," he said, "we would gain nothing but to entail bankruptcy on every individual whose property was brought under the hammer." The depression had left Arkansas with no money, slave prices had fallen seventy-five percent and land prices ninety percent. The only hope for eastern bondholders would be to wait a few years for prosperity to return and then perhaps the planters would be willing to resume paying interest and maybe even the principal.[8]

While eastern bond holders and the Arkansas public credit were ruined, the planters were to be protected. Planters had their twenty-year loans and freedom from responsibility for any bank debts except their own. Even as the popular outcry for public liquidation of the bank grew, the planters arranged continued financial protection for themselves. They were not to be outmaneuvered by the hillcountry representative, Archibald Yell, who voiced the public outrage against banking. The congressman from Fayetteville was a natural politician who could lead the church singing, shout the loudest in the Amen corner, and then outdrink and outshoot the unchurched good old boys. He had speculated himself and owned shares of the bank but quickly shifted with popular antibank sentiment and won election in 1840 as governor on an antibanking platform. Yell seemed intent on closing the banks and liquidating their holdings. He developed a legal position that the Real Estate Bank had violated its charter by defaulting on the bond interest, mortgaging the Holford bonds, and attempting to deceive the legislature. Despite Yell's antibank rhetoric, no action followed until the shrewd planters had transferred their banking assets to a trust, in 1842, and elected their own trustees—the old bank officials who would never press them to repay their debts. The courts sustained the bank maneuver and for thirteen years the planter trustees and politicians protected themselves and their class. Not until prosperity and its flush times returned in the 1850s, allowing the Conway-Sevier-Johnson family to pay its debts, was the state government permitted to take control of the bank assets.

The public then learned much of the truth about plantation banking. The trustees had collected only enough money to pay their own salaries. Payment had been accepted in depreciated state bonds and bank paper, thus allowing planters to reduce their debts by as much as half. Even then the directors had paid little or nothing; their twenty-year mortgages were not yet due, only the nonstockholders with their ten-year mortgages had been requested to repay their debts.

The bank had surely assisted the growth of the planter class. Consider the development of Chicot County, the flat delta land stretching along the Mississippi River in the extreme southeast corner of the state, just north of Louisiana. In 1830 fewer than a thousand whites could be found on this rich delta jungle, and most of them were squatters living along the river. Ten years later, after the establishment of the bank, the white population had grown by only 200 but the black population increased by almost 2500 and turned the county into a major cotton producer. The entire state of Arkansas had produced only 15,000 bales of cotton in 1840 but two years later bank president Anthony J. Davies estimated that his county alone would produce that number of bales.[10]

Davies, the author of the plantation banking legislation, was a self-made man who had left his Connecticut home at the age of twelve. The young entrepreneur moved to the southwest in search of a fortune as a bookkeeper and merchandiser. He arrived in Little Rock in 1830 and five years later moved on to undeveloped Chicot County as a planter and merchant. With his bank loan of $15,000 he prospered. When Arkansas took over the bank assets in 1855 Davies owed $23,444.49; but he had obviously put the money to more profitable use than paying off the debt, because he could boast to the 1860 census taker that his worth amounted to $278,000 including the Lake Village plantation with its 145 slaves. Davies' neighbors prospered, too; they held more slaves than planters in any other county, an average of 33.3 slaves, and included the state's largest slaveholder, Elisha Worthington with 528 slaves.[11]

The Real Estate Bank undeniably assisted in creating a wealthy planter class. Eastern capital helped to finance the importation of 15,000 slaves during the 1830s, raising the number of blacks by 500 percent and increasing their share of the state population to twenty percent. Slaves went to the rich fever-infested lowlands which white settlers avoided for the healthier hill country. As slave labor cleared and planted the bottom lands Arkansas emerged as a major cotton producer. The bank-financed planters proved that the plantation could thrive in Arkansas and thus encouraged planters from the older states to emigrate. The annual cotton crop grew from 15,058 bales in 1840 to 367,395 in 1860, making Arkansas the sixth largest cotton producer. To be sure, small white upland farmers grew much of that cotton but the slaves, which made up one-fourth of the population, produced half of the crop.

The Arkansas investment in plantations produced an economic elite of 500 who committed the state to the evils of human slavery which would be ended only by the horrors of war and revolution. But even if the questions of morality could be ignored, the economic consequences for the general population must still be judged damaging. Investments in plantations did not assist the general welfare as money spent for transportation or education might have done. If Arkansas farmers were to diversify their crops, they required railroads for rapid shipping of fruits and vegetables. If lumber and mineral resources were to be exploited, railroads were also essential. The steam locomotive could have benefitted the general population but Arkansas was unable to finance a single railroad because she had ruined her credit rating by repudiating the Holford Bonds and defaulting annually on the interest of the other state securities. Of course, cotton planters did not especially need railroads, steam boats were adequate for their crops and so Arkansas built only 28 miles of track by 1860 while her sister state Michigan had constructed 799 miles.

Investment in children through public education was almost universally approved in America except in Arkansas, the only state before the Civil War without a school tax. Planter politicians had talked of schools and even consented to establishing a school law in 1843 but never voted a state school tax. Even though the federal government gave the state nearly a million acres of land to finance a university, the antebellum politicians created no college but used the money collected for general revenues. Some of the education money from land sales did go to private elementary schools but not enough to provide free public education. What Arkansas called public schools required tuition payments just as did the private academies. Education in Arkansas consisted of 836 one-room, one-teacher schools, and 109 academies with 1.5 teachers each. These schools were in operation only four months of each year. Inadequate education and the other consequences of the planter swindle would continue long past the Civil War.[12]

4

The Civil War

The elimination of slavery required Arkansas to suffer her greatest tragedy. Four years of violence left the landscape dotted with gaunt blackened chimneys, broken fences, shattered lives, and freshly dug graves. The pain would surely have been less if Arkansas had united on either side of the war, but she divided her loyalties. Planters of the lowlands who had migrated from Virginia, Tennessee, and the Carolinas were outspoken advocates of the Confederacy, while the hill people from the mountains of Tennessee, along with the town people from northern states, were often Unionists.[1] Partisan violence among her own citizens, painful outside invasion, and prolonged foreign occupation combined to create hatreds persisting for more than a century.

A majority of Arkansans initially opposed secession. As in other border states, loyalty to the Union remained strong even after the deep South states organized the Confederate States of America. Arkansans elected a loyal majority to their state convention and rejected secession in February 1861 by a vote of thirty-nine to thirty-five. But the inevitability of war had already been predicted by Albert Pike, Boston-born poet and Little Rock attorney. This former Unionist knew that the northern Congress offered no compromise

27

acceptable to the seceded states and therefore the choice for Arkansas had been reduced: "to go voluntarily out of the Union, to be dropped out or kicked out." Then President Lincoln's call for troops from Arkansas, after South Carolina's attack on Fort Sumter, shifted the majority behind the secessionist planter-politicians. Governor Henry M. Rector replied to federal request with the planter's intemperate language:

> In answer to your requisition for troops from Arkansas, to subjugate the southern States, I have to say that none will be furnished. The demand is only adding insult to injury. The people of this Commonwealth are freemen, not slaves, and will defend to the last extremity their honor, lives and property against northern mendacity and usurpation.[2]

President Lincoln's decision to force the seceded states back into the Union created a reluctant majority in Arkansas for the Confederacy. Many former Unionists explained their decision not as a defense of slavery or states rights but as a simple decision to side with friends and relatives. The North appeared the aggressor while the deep South states intended Arkansas no harm. As a Unionist delegate, William Stout from the hillcountry of Pope County, explained: he loved the United States flag, believed it was the President's duty to put down rebellion, and could never be devoted to the "cotton confederacy" but neither could he take up the Northern gun and begin killing his Southern brothers who "never did me any harm and never intend to do me any." So Stout and many other Unionists became reluctant Confederates, now voting with the militant secessionists, such as Governor Rector, who had asserted: "God in His omnipotent wisdom . . . created the cotton plant—the African slave—and the lower Mississippi valley, to clothe and feed the world, and a gallant race of men and women produced upon its soil to defend it, and execute that decree." When the state convention convened a second time to reconsider secession, only five Unionists opposed the planter-politicians who led Arkansas out of the Union on May 6, 1861.[3]

Secessionists sought unanimity of opinion throughout the state but never entirely enforced their command. Even in the secession convention one man, Isaac Murphy from Madison County, refused to change his vote and make unanimous the decision to secede.

Vigilante groups suppressed Union sentiments in southeast Arkansas, inducing most adult males to support the Confederacy, but in the northwest, as few as 16 percent volunteered in Madison County, a secret Peace Society organized, and 8289 volunteers enlisted on the Northern side when Union armies later marched through the hillcountry. Perhaps fifteen percent of white Arkansas males fought for the Union side, along with 5526 Arkansas blacks, in opposition to the more than 50,000 state Confederates.[4]

The split over secession dampened conversation among hillcountry neighbors. As a north Arkansas girl recalled:

> The day of frank expression was past. Persons looked askance at those they met. A friend of yesterday might be a foe of today; so men looked into the faces of the other men with questioning eye and words were carefully chosen. Even children had been taught a silent caution, listening but saying little.

Those who chose loyalty to the nation kept their Fourth of July celebration quiet, as did Jonas Tebbetts who, on the evening of Independence Day, called his children into a candle-lit room to conduct a solemn ceremony before an American flag.

> Children, this is the fourth of July, 1861. I want you to remember that you heard your father read the 'Declaration of Independence' on this day; and it is my wish that you either read aloud or hear aloud this great paper on every fourth of July that comes into your life. Also, I want you to remember that during this stress of war and danger, your father and mother are still loyal to this flag before you and to the government for which it stands.[5]

In the initial Confederate outburst of war enthusiasm south Arkansas sent two infantry regiments east to join the Confederate armies, including a private from Helena—Patrick R. Cleburne—who would become the state's most distinguished soldier. Arkansas sent a third brigade north into Missouri where Confederate sympathizers were being pushed toward Arkansas. Led by Sterling "Old Pap" Price, the Confederate Missouri State Guard finally stood at Wilson's Creek where, reinforced by troops from Arkansas, Texas, and Louisiana, they routed the Federal army and killed its commander.[6]

The military fortunes of Missouri and Arkansas Confederates were bound together. So long as Price successfully resisted Federal armies, Arkansas would be spared from invasion. The battle of Wilson's Creek kept the war from Arkansas for another seven months but then a new Federal army pushed Price into Arkansas for the major battle to determine dominance of the West. The importance of Arkansas and Missouri, though recognized by Confederate president Jefferson Davis, brought no army of reinforcement from the East. Davis sent only a general, Earl Van Dorn, a dapper Mississippi-born and West Point–trained soldier. Van Dorn rushed to Pea Ridge, hurried his 16,000 men into an unwise assault on a smaller Federal army and lost the battle of Pea Ridge (March 6–8, 1862), leaving northwest Arkansas occupied by the Federals.[7]

After the battle of Pea Ridge, the Confederate command abandoned Arkansas. Generals Van Dorn and Price were ordered east to defend Mississippi and Tennessee against General U.S. Grant. Arkansas had to be sacrificed. So Arkansas Confederate troops moved east, across the Mississippi River, leaving their state defenseless. Governor Henry M. Rector grew so livid with rage that he talked of seceding from the Confederacy. Only after the victorious Federal army from Pea Ridge approached within thirty-five miles of the state capital did Confederate General Thomas C. Hindman assume command to hold Arkansas for the South. Hindman was a five-foot-two-inch bundle of energy who had been a Helena lawyer, a congressman, and an early secessionist. When the war began he raised a volunteer regiment and led it across the Mississippi to fight in Kentucky. Hindman now assumed dictatorial powers in Arkansas, declared martial law, and encouraged guerrilla warfare by authorizing the formation of independent companies of irregulars. "Resist the enemy to the last extremity," he insisted, "blockading roads, burning bridges, destroying all supplies, growing crops included, and polluting the water by killing cattle, ripping the carcasses, and throwing them in."[8] Hindman, it seems, would destroy the land and make life miserable for its people in order to save Arkansas for the Confederacy.

Hindman raised an army for the second attempt to recapture northwest Arkansas from the Federals. He marched his army of 10,000 up the valley of the Arkansas, across the Boston Mountains, and fought the Union army of the frontier to a stalemate. But after exhausting all supplies of food and ammunition, Hindman left his dead and wounded, thirteen percent of the army, and retreated back over the Boston Mountains, leaving northern Arkansas to the Union and the door open for the Federals to capture the capital at Little Rock.[9]

Again the Confederacy sent generals—Sterling Price and Edmund Kirby Smith—but no troops. The generals, outmaneuvered by a larger Federal army led by Frederick Steele, abandoned the state capital without even a battle. The Confederate troops retreated from Little Rock on September 10, 1863, falling back to the southwest corner of the state. The establishment of a new Confederate state capital in the town of Washington only confirmed that Arkansas Confederates had lost control of most of the state.

In east Arkansas the Federals under Generals Curtis and Steele had moved down the White River in the summer of 1862 capturing the plantation towns from Batesville to Helena. With the capture of Arkansas Post that winter, the plantations of Arkansas fell into Union hands, along with many of the freedmen who, when given a chance, left slavery. As one ex-slave said, "like when you leave de lot gate open where is a big litter of shotes and dey just hit de road and commence to ramble. Mos of em, dey go on to Helena and gets dey grub from de Yankees." Under the Federals blacks could become soldiers or work for wages. A Federal experiment in free labor, on plantations deserted by Confederate owners, persuaded Federal officials by 1864 that free blacks could succeed either as wage laborers or as renters who managed their own cotton crop.[10]

While the war continued for two more years law and order could not be established outside the rival Federal and Confederate garrisons. Guerrilla warfare conducted by rival bands of irregulars, along with lawless bushwhackers and jayhawkers, plundered and killed the unprotected population. Even the regular armies conducted foraging expeditions, appropriating food and forage just as irregulars and guerrillas did. By 1865 the smoke-houses as well as the land had been stripped, actual starvation seemed widespread, and the last months of the war were impressed on folk memories as "the year of the famine."[11]

Arkansas Unionists had emerged after the Federal victories of

1862 to seek political control of their state and follow President Lincoln's requirements for rebuilding loyal governments. They were led by Isaac Murphy, the single delegate to the Arkansas Convention of 1861 who had refused to vote for secession. The fifty-seven-year-old, Pennsylvania-born, schoolteacher-lawyer had first intended to sit out the war where he had lived for almost thirty years. But even in the mountain town of Huntsville Confederate partisans forced Murphy to either join the South or move. He and his neighbor James M. Johnson fled north to join the Union armies in Missouri. There General Samuel R. Curtis took the elderly Murphy as a civilian member of his staff for the campaign across Arkansas. In early 1863 Murphy wrote to the president of the United States, applauding his Emancipation Proclamation and offering to lead the Arkansas movement to restore loyal government and establish freedom. "I now devote myself," he promised, "to the cause of my country and of human liberty and am anxious to serve."[12]

The nonslaveholding Murphy was a man of modest wealth before the war, $600 in real estate and $700 in personal property, who hated both slavery and the wealthy slaveholders. His anger had risen as wealthy rebels hastened to win favor from the triumphant Union soldiers in Little Rock. He bitterly resented the attention which Federal officers were giving to the rich and formerly disloyal Arkansans. "Wealthy rebels invite the high officers to their houses," Murphy complained, "introduce them to their families, tickle them with flattering attentions, and soften them with delusive blandishments . . . . The common result is that the worst Rebels are protected . . . and favored—and the Union men true and Loyal crushed down by the misrepresentation of traitors—double dyed & damned traitors. The wealthy polished traitor Lie has more influence than the honest truth from the rough and poor man."[13]

The homespun-clad Murphy determined to see wealthy traitors dishonored and Union loyalty exhalted. He followed the Union army to Little Rock, participated in the movement to hold a constitutional convention, and won election as provisional governor when the Union delegates assembled in Little Rock on January 4, 1864, to reorganize state government without slavery. After the new constitution and the governor were ratified by twenty percent of the eligible voters, more than double the Lincoln requirement,

Murphy delivered his inaugural address on April 18, rejoicing in a "Free Arkansas," purified of the sin of human slavery and destined to be sustained if the citizens supported his pure Christian principles and his plans for a sound public school system.

Governor Murphy knew his to be a minority government enforced only by Union armies. He pressed Lincoln to continue military protection for the government and the loyal citizens. "Should the Army leave," he informed Lincoln "terror will prevail." Guerrillas and armed bands infested the countryside and the new government had no money to organize a local militia fo protecting the courts and suppressing theft, rape, and murder. More than a year of violence continued before Murphy could finally announce on May 10, 1865, "the war is over."[14]

The fighting had inflicted punishing casualties on Arkansas and the other Confederate states. Virtually every able-bodied male had participated in the war and now one-fourth of them were either dead or incapacitated. Every family now mourned the loss of a father, a son, a cousin, an uncle or a brother. All had been hurt by the war and most now suffered the humiliation of being on the losing side, beaten by the Yankees and Republicans. Governor Murphy wisely avoided the arrogance of a victor, making instead an offer of forgiveness:

> We have all done wrong. No one can say that his heart is altogether clean, and his hands pure. Then, as we wish to be forgiven, let us forgive those who have sinned against us, and ours.
>
> The land is steeped in blood—innocent blood—and defiled with crime. Let us wash it out with tears of sorrow and repentance, works of love, kindness and charity, that peace, goodwill and confidence may return and dwell among us.
>
> Let our last conquest be the conquest of the hearts of our enemies by kindness—then peace will be lasting.[15]

Murphy's eloquence won praise even from the rebels and gave the governor a reputation as a statesman—one who inspires men to be better than they really are. Charity and kindness, however, were not the emotions felt by returning rebel refugees such as Susan Briceland Fletcher, who observed: "Desolation met our gaze; abandoned and burned homes; half starved women and children; gaunt, ragged men, stumbling along the road . . . trying to find their

families and friends. . . . We found our home burned to the ground."
Nor could the conquering Federals muster much affection for their
ex-foes. "I don't like a Rebel," Minos Miller reported to his mother,
"and never expect to, and every man in this country who has been
a Rebel is a Rebel yet and they are showing it every day."[16]

For only one short summer Arkansans restrained their anger
and followed Governor Murphy's call for peace. They cleared the
brush from the fields, rebuilt the fences, and planted a crop with
seed from the Freedmen's Bureau. All were tired of war but neither
repentant nor willing to forgive those who had been their enemies.
When the crops were harvested, and hunger satisfied, revenge and
violence were certain to follow.

Governor Murphy generously approved individual pardon ap-
plications for former influential Confederates, but he retained Union
political control by enforcing an election loyalty oath which disfranchised all who had supported the Confederacy during the last
two years of the war. These disfranchised Confederates began to
emerge from the shock of defeat by the fall of 1865 and to assert
their claims for political rights against the Murphy government which
did not represent the will of the Arkansas majority. The first political assassinations of Union county officials began in the backcountry in the fall of 1865. While some sought revenge through political
violence, most ex-rebels joined the nonviolent effort to regain
political control of their state and local government. When the
Arkansas Supreme Court agreed with the ex-rebels in December
1865 that the Murphy legislature could not restrict the democratic
suffrage by a loyalty oath, the way was open for a nonviolent
overthrow of the Union government.

5

Carpetbaggers

A war for control of Arkansas continued nine years beyond the defeat of the Confederacy. The humiliated Confederates were unwilling to leave government in the hands of their Union conquerors. Labeling themselves "Conservatives," the ex-rebels organized and fought with bullets as well as ballots for almost a decade before finally retaking state and local government. Even after the final victory in 1874, so extreme were hostilities that another hundred years passed before these Confederate-Conservative-Democratic winners consented to allow the portrait of the carpetbag Republican governor—Powell Clayton—to be displayed in the state capitol along with all the other governors.[1] Not until the present generation did political passions cool sufficiently for Arkansans to consider Reconstruction without antagonism.

The first ex-rebel move to recapture Arkansas won control of the state legislature in 1866. In the elections of that year Conservative voters ousted virtually every Unionist. And while the newly elected legislature drafted no black codes to bind freedmen back into slavery, it blatantly expressed thanks to Jefferson Davis for his rebel leadership, voted pensions for ex-Confederate soldiers, rejected the Fourteenth Amendment, and moved to impeach Unionist circuit judges. The angry Republican Congress, fearful that its victory over rebellion and slavery might be lost, moved against Arkansas and the other southern state governments in February 1867, placing these states under military rule, suspending civil government, and requiring new state constitutional conventions which would establish black suffrage. Democrat-Conservatives were thus deprived of their election victory, forced from state office, and compelled to watch the local Republican-Unionists reestablish loyal rule.[2]

Young Republicans from the North now provided the loyal initiative. They had come to Arkansas as Federal officers and stayed on after the war to engage in law or cotton planting. Powell Clayton, a young civil engineer from New York and Kansas, had come to Arkansas as a Union cavalry officer, bought a plantation near Pine Bluff, married a local girl, and grown angry as Confederate neighbors vandalized his property. Clayton and other tough-minded Unionists, who believed the Murphy government had been too soft, now assumed leadership of the new Republican effort to write a fresh constitution, establish law and order, and enact Yankee reforms.[3]

Clayton and his fellow carpetbaggers were young men in their thirties, convinced that they and their new party were spokesmen of progress and reform. They were participants in a movement which would bring not only equality for blacks but also economic modernization and industrial growth to backward Arkansas. The carpetbaggers numbered only seventeen of the seventy delegates to the Constitutional Convention of 1868, but with their superior zeal and the votes of the eight black delegates they controlled more votes than the native Unionists and thus controlled both the state constitutional convention and the Republican convention which nominated candidates for state office. After the more numerous Democrats failed to defeat the new Republican constitution (many ex-Confederates were denied the ballot when they were either unable or unwilling to persuade the Republican voting registrars of their loyalty), Democrats did not even contest the following elections and Powell Clayton became governor of the first southern state permitted by Congress to emerge from military reconstruction.[4]

On July 2, 1868, the old, homespun-clad Murphy turned Arkansas over to a young, fashionably attired Clayton determined to establish a Republican order. Clayton respected Murphy's honesty but disdained what he considered the weakness of the old government. He intended to organize a loyal militia to suppress violence and then push for rapid economic development. Clayton asserted that economic growth required railroads. The locomotive was the great engine of progress which brought immigrants and would give Arkansas the necessary increase in population. Railroads would stimulate every branch of industry. Wherever the locomotive whistled, he said, "forests disappear, the rough face of nature is smoothed down, and farms, villages, towns, and cities spring up as if by magic."[5]

Democrats shared Clayton's passion for railroads, even anticipating his financial plans for promoting railroad construction. The Democratic legislature of 1866 had voted to restore the state credit and sell railroad bonds. Under Clayton, Arkansas would exchange the 1830s bank bonds for new bonds, demonstrating a willingness to pay the defaulted state debt. Having thus agreed to repay the old $3 million debt, the state could go into the bond market and sell $5 million of railroad bonds to finance 420 miles of track crisscrossing Arkansas. Democrats complained not of the principal plans but only of refunding the Holford bonds. This $500,000 should not be considered a just part of the state debt, they said, because the old Real Estate Bank officials had illegally mortgaged the bonds to a New York banking firm and the firm in turn had illegally sold the bonds to the British investor James Holford. But the Democratic objections were overriden and Clayton refunded the entire state debt.

New state financing pushed railroad construction forward and at the close of Republican rule counted more than 400 miles of track assisted by the state aid of $5,350,000 in bonds. State aid completed the Memphis and Little Rock line and virtually completed the Little Rock to Fort Smith road. At the same time a privately financed Cairo and Fulton railroad built a line across the state from the northeast to Texarkana without even asking for state-guaranteed bonds. Together, private capitalism and state bond money developed a railroad system for every section except the northwest.[6]

The carpetbaggers also established free public education. Republicans considered free schools to be as important as free labor and railroads in bringing Arkansas into the mainstream of western civilization. The past neglect of education had produced ignorant citizens who permitted the misrule of the planter class. One-third of the white voters, Clayton asserted, could not even write their own names. If free government were to prevail, blacks and whites must be instructed. And the Republicans did build more than a thousand free schools and opened the University of Arkansas at Fayetteville.[7]

Least successful of the Clayton programs were the levee bonds. The former engineer and Pine Bluff planter had shared the optimists' assumption that man could alter the annual spring flood. Since 1849 the official policy of both state and federal government had been to support levee construction with public funds. But each decade witnessed one or two flood years in which the rivers rose above the levees, causing more damage than an unrestricted river. For almost a hundred years money and resources were wasted before the Mississippi and lower Arkansas were tamed. Governor Clayton contributed to this foolishness by issuing levee bonds in 1869 which increased the state's indebtedness by $2.3 million and damaged the state credit rating, while building few levees.

Reformers are rarely appreciated and certainly Clayton won little applause for his innovations. Democratic Arkansans regarded the Clayton administration as an evil imposed on the state. No Yankee outsider, and especially one elected by black voters while many whites were disqualified from voting, could have won acceptance. The carpetbaggers were viewed as Yankee oppressors, out to exploit the state for personal profit. Clayton had even been a murdering tyrant, it was said, calling out the militia to kill loyal Democrats.

On coming to office, Governor Clayton had resolved to protect Union men. Distressing murders of both black and white Union men occurred in a dozen counties in the summer and fall of 1868. The governor's agent, sent to investigate the secret Ku Klux Klan, was murdered in White County. Newly elected carpetbag congressman James M. Hinds was assassinated in Monroe County on October 22, and state representative Joseph Brooks wounded while going to speak at a political meeting. When the U.S. Secretary of War refused to provide assistance in suppressing domestic violence, Clayton believed he had no acceptable alternative. On November 4 he declared martial law in ten counties, suspending civil law and calling out the militia to put down all conspiracies to overthrow Union government.[8]

Martial law offered an emotional target for every critic. A militia can be easy to criticize if the state has no money to supply the soldiers and permits them to live off the land, confiscating chickens, hams, and horses from Democratic farmers along with guns and supplies from local stores. Receipts and hastily contrived vouchers, of course, were given by the militia, but who willingly exchanges valued goods for promises to pay some day? And who likes to see political enemies with guns arresting and executing men without a jury trial? The handful of executions, following militia court martials, were less criticized than the shooting of prisoners who were said to be resisting or attempting to escape. But even more emotional was the use of black militia under white officers (about 60 percent of the militia was black). Three white women were raped by black soldiers and, even though the guilty individuals were executed by their fellow soldiers, no Democrat forgave Clayton for calling out the militia or for enrolling blacks in it.

Clayton's three months of martial law may have broken up Klan organizations and been partially effective in establishing fear and respect for the Republican administration, but it also seems to have been a political mistake. Even within the Republican party many regarded Clayton's use of the militia as an abuse of his constitutional powers. Some native Republicans—such as Lieutenant Governor James M. Johnson, who had always resented an outsider becoming governor—moved into opposition. Johnson, a physician from Madison County who had organized a Union cavalry regiment during the war, represented those northwest Republicans whose section had received no railroad and none of the benefits from Clayton's $3 million levee bond scheme to protect delta lands from floods. Naturally the Clayton administration appeared too extravagant in its economic plans. During the militia controversy Johnson moved into open opposition to Clayton's administration, linking excessive use of force with excessive financial extravagance in his criticism of the administration.[9]

Republican critics were not all native Arkansans. Joseph Brooks had the best of carpetbag credentials. A Methodist minister and abolitionist who edited a St. Louis antislavery paper, he first came to Arkansas as chaplain to a black regiment. After the war he remained in the state as a cotton planter and active Republican. This forceful Republican orator became the leading voice calling for less government, restricting the powers of the governor, and restricting fiscal extravagance. Brooks appealed to black voters, promising to protect their rights, and to white Democrats, promising to abolish restrictions on voting. He sought to redraw party lines, calling himself a Liberal Republican and those in power the Radical Republicans.[10]

Clayton easily retained the loyalty of predominately black counties but his power began to erode in white upland counties such as Pope, a western county which ran north of the Arkansas River into the Ozark Mountains. Only a few blacks lived in this 93 percent white county and thus the political struggle occurred between white Unionists and the more numerous white Democrats. Civil War bitterness had persisted in Pope as Democrats assassinated the county officials appointed by Governor Murphy in 1865–66. Military reconstruction enabled a carpetbag supporter of Clayton to establish control of local government. Wallace H. Hickox, a bold twenty-eight-year-old sergeant from Illinois who had become a local cotton planter, was appointed as an election registrar in 1868, giving him the opportunity to become county clerk and the leading local Republican. Hickox rode the best horse in Pope County, kept two of the better looking women, and called local Democrats "damned rebels."[11]

Hickox could control the county by vote fraud so long as local Republicans, who composed one-third of the population, cooperated. Defections to the Liberal Republican opposition in 1872 threatened to overthrow the Hickox regime. In a desperate attempt to secure martial law and a reelection, Hickox shot two prisoners and reported to the governor that an uprising of rebels was out of hand. Pope County did in fact become an armed camp and assassinations multiplied, bringing in the state guard and permitting another manipulated election, although Hickox did not live to see the Republican victory, having been shot down in the street of Dover. The local Democratic guerrilla war overturned the election results by killing the elected Republican county officers. By 1873 the day of the carpetbagger was over in Pope County and all of

Arkansas. The Democratic majority no longer tolerated rule by outsiders.

Reconstruction in Arkansas ended with less violence outside of Pope County because Clayton had moved on to the U.S. Senate, leaving the state under Governor Elisha Baxter. Clayton's manipulated election of 1872 gave the victory to Baxter over the Liberal Republican-Democratic candidate Joseph Brooks, but Baxter then deserted the carpetbaggers and switched his loyalties to the Democrats. Outraged Republicans turned to Brooks, whom they had fraudulently counted out in the last election but now sought to use for expelling Baxter. For a time, in 1874, a Brooks-Baxter war threatened as armed forces gathered in Little Rock. But when the U.S. Congress declined to intervene for Brooks, the dominant Democrats were left in power and Reconstruction was officially over.

"All hail, happy day," Democrats rejoiced. Though they spoke of charity in victory, urged toleration of blacks and Republicans, and adopted legislation prohibiting the carrying of knives and guns in public, Democrats could not resist political mythmaking to blacken the reputation of Republican reconstruction. Each decade further embellished the tales of outrage until state historians took over denunciation of the "alien, wasteful, corrupt, vindictive" Republican rule. No reconstruction reform went unscathed: all were condemned as schemes to exploit and squander—even free public education. Republicans were vilified for increasing the state debt from $3 to $16 million with "no return, except despotic government, broken credit, ruined industry, a deplorable corruption of public morals."[12]

While it is true that young carpetbaggers had been reckless with state credit, they did provide Arkansas with a railroad system. And even though Democrats failed to thank the Republicans, they later attributed Arkansas's progress to the locomotive. As Ben T. DuVal told the old timers at Prairie Grove on July 4, 1884:

> With the advent of railroads and telegraph, old Arkansas disappears, the dirt road and slow coaches have vanished. The easy, somewhat indolent life of the first settlers is superseded by the activity which rapid travel promotes. New industries are called into existence by the development of natural resources. A stream of immigration has poured into our borders, a new population

who with quick and eager hands turn the treasures of the forest, the soil and mines into money. The early settlers and their descendants must quicken their steps or yield to the coming tide, and go.[13]

Railroads tied Arkansas to the nation and made economic diversification possible. Strawberries, apples, and peaches could now be grown for the northern markets. Lumber could be transported to the world and become the state's major industry. Railroads would bring in a larger population, sprinkling a few Germans, Swiss, and Italian settlements among the Scotch, English, and African. The Arkansas population of 484,471 in 1870 jumped to 802,525 in 1880 and climbed to 1,113,775 in 1890.

Economic growth never restored the state credit. The reconstruction bonds had become a political issue and in 1884 Arkansas repudiated much of its debt, as did seven other southern states. Arkansas repudiated the railroad, the levee, and the Holford bonds, leaving only the original bank bonds which were redeemed at depreciated market prices. Needless to say, Arkansas ruined its credit in the financial world, but few of her citizens cared because they accepted the Democratic story that corrupt carpetbaggers had unjustly imposed the bonds by fraud.

6

Black Man's Place

After a decade of freedom blacks believed their place in Arkansas firmly established. They now worked fewer hours than under slavery and they had the freedom to live as did white folks on a single family farm, to vote, to hold public office, and to enjoy equal access to public accommodations. None could have remained unfamiliar with freedom after a decade of schooling by northern missionaries, Republican politicians, the Freedmen's Bureau, and the black ministers. Every community enjoyed its politics, its school, and its church.

An exhilarating contact with the outside world, begun by the liberating Union armies, had continued with white missionary teachers from the northern Methodists, Quakers, Presbyterians, and Congregationalists. Missionary schools opened in all the major population centers. Black missionaries came, too. The African Methodist Episcopal Church established congregations in 1864, bringing Arkansas blacks into the northern denomination. After 1870 the Colored Methodist Episcopal Church from Tennessee recruited for the second black Methodist denomination. To be sure, most blacks were Baptists with no national church hierarchy to call, but even Baptists enjoyed a voluntary influx of outside ministers. Two black carpetbaggers, James T. White and William H. Grey, set-

43

tled in Helena as religious and political leaders, offering the most outspoken advocacy of equality in the Arkansas Constitutional Convention of 1868. Grey had observed sessions of the national Congress and used his acquired knowledge of parliamentary procedure to win acclaim as the ablest black delegate to the Arkansas Constitutional Convention. Grey pushed the principles of the Declaration of Independence—all men are created free and equal. The current ignorance of blacks was only a temporary condition, he said, for those who had been carried to America "hatless, coatless, shoeless and naked." When given education and equal civil rights, he promised, blacks would prove themselves capable of civilization and enlightenment.[1]

Grey optimistically promoted Arkansas as a land of opportunity for blacks. He persuaded attorney M.W. Gibbs to settle in Arkansas, where he became the first black elected to a judgeship in the United States. Gibbs had begun life in Philadelphia in 1823, followed the gold rush to California, prospered as a western merchant, and then returned to Oberlin College; he moved on to Little Rock in 1871. Two years later he won election as municipal judge of Little Rock. In addition to Gibbs's judgeship, blacks held half of the seats on the Little Rock city council and seats for ten counties in the state legislature. In counties with black majorities, such as Chicot, Phillips, Crittenden, and Jefferson, they dominated local government, serving as sheriffs, county clerks, and tax assessors.[2]

Politics had opened for blacks with the beginning of Congressional Reconstruction in 1867. That summer blacks turned out for July 4 political rallies and barbecues across the state. Marching under the sponsorship of white Republicans and under their own banner, "Our Guide the Bible and the Constitution," they assembled for readings of the Declaration of Independence and the Emancipation Proclamation as well as radical Republican promises to sponsor railroads, free schools, and racial equality in return for political support from black people. Those promises were kept. Black men voted, schools were built, and an Arkansas Civil Rights law guaranteed equality in public places.

While blacks believed their political equality permanent, white Democrats refused to accept legal equality as more than temporary. Democrats denigrated blacks as a primitive race—"poor, deluded, ignorant, superstitious creatures"—to be deprived of social and political equality so that white supremacy might survive in the delta counties. Black Power, they said, had led to such horrors as the Chicot County troubles. The trouble began in a Lake Village grocery in December 1871 where three whites complained of the recent voting referendum in which black voters supported a county bond issue of $250,000 to finance a railroad running west to Texas. A black attorney intervened in the discussion, defending the additional taxation, but was attacked and killed with a knife. The three white men were promptly arrested for murder. On the following weekend a black mob took the white prisoners from jail, gunned them down, and then looted the grocery and other property of the three men. "We ain't gwine to hab no more damn white trash in Chicot County," they were reported to have said. "Dis country belongs to de cullud man, you bet." White men, fearing the worst, rushed their women out of the county. No further violence occurred but neither did the leading black official, James W. Mason, the wealthy illegitimate son of a white planter, prosecute the members of the black mob. In fact, Mason seemed to have encouraged the shootings and, as county judge and sheriff, prevented prosecutions. Mob violence and abuse of power in Arkansas were not without precedent, but white Democrats regarded the Chicot affair as more horrible because they believed it to have been committed by an ignorant and inferior African race put in power by Republicans who turned society wrong side up.[3]

White Democratic leadership, always committed to disfranchising blacks, recognized the impossibility of ending black political power immediately. To avoid federal intervention, any movement against black power had to proceed with caution. So the Democratic leadership sought to reassure blacks in 1874, asking their support and promising to defend all political rights. Many blacks recognized the demise of white Republican power and negotiated white endorsement of racially integrated tickets in exchange for black support of the new state constitution in 1874. The delighted Democratic press assured blacks that "they need never fear but that their rights will be protected."[4]

Black labor had been much in demand along the delta where planters offered $15 to $25 a month, double the wages paid in South

Carolina or Georgia. Planters surely wished to make Arkansas attractive for immigration and the black population grew by 72.4 percent, from 122,169 to 210,666 during the seventies. After planters shifted from paying wages to offering sharecrop contracts, their agents traveled throughout the older southeastern states offering transportation to virgin Arkansas land. Agents seem to have boasted not only of bale-and-a-half an acre land but also of sweet potatoes as large as watermelons, trees which grew paper money, fritter ponds, and even barbecued hogs walking around with knives and forks attached. Free schools and civil rights were also part of the sales pitch which brought thousands of blacks from the older states to delta plantations. Once in Arkansas, of course, the state fell far short of the Promised Land. Even the transportation proved not to be free but an expense added to the debt binding the sharecropper to the plantation. Nor did the planters and the Arkansas legislature hesitate to move harshly against black crime by abolishing the distinction between grand and petit larceny, making a $2 theft a pententiary offense. In each county the convicts were leased to the highest bidder, creating a form of slavery for those convicted of stealing a pig. Still blacks came by the thousands throughout the 1880s.[5]

The Democratic promise to protect black political rights lasted less than four years before the first serious moves against black power occurred. Jefferson County Democrats overcame a 3000-vote Republican majority and returned to power in 1878 by manipulating voting returns and bribing black leaders. Phillips County Democrats took advantage of a yellow fever quarantine to organize militia companies, disrupt black political rallies, prevent blacks from voting, and end Republican rule. Black power in Arkansas had seriously eroded after only four years of Democratic state control.[6]

Ten years later an even more flagrant use of force in Crittenden County marked the final end of respect for black political rights. Just across the river from Memphis, Tennessee, blacks outnumbered whites by five to one. Blacks had controlled elections in Crittenden County for twenty years, although in recent campaigns they permitted whites a token position—sheriff—while they held all others until 1888. Then whites determined to end black political power. First, a committee obtained fifty Winchester rifles and a supply of ammunition from Memphis, and then, in a meeting with much handclapping and foot stamping, announced plans for expelling the black leadership. On the morning of July 13 twenty-one blacks in Marion, including holders of public office, journalists, and ministers, were driven out of town. As county court clerk Dave Ferguson said, "I was at work in my office in the courthouse Thursday morning, when in stepped eighty white men armed with Winchesters. They said, 'Ferguson, this county is too small for you and us. You'll have to leave.'" The county clerk and the other twenty were marched down to the railroad station and put on the train for Memphis with one-way tickets. When these Marion exiles petitioned Governor Simon Hughes for protection, he claimed no power to intervene. The white seizure of Crittenden thus went unchallenged.[7]

Even some carpetbag Republicans accepted the white revolution. As federal judge John McClure explained to the Little Rock Lincoln Club, black political power had been a mistake because it created the fear of black domination. Southern whites never accepted black rule and the citizens of Crittenden County had only followed the example of white Mississippi, Louisiana, and South Carolina. Nothing could be done for black Marion exiles because the law could not be enforced against white public sentiment. "Men in Crittenden were tired of Negro rule," McClure said. "They threw it off. Public sentiment will sustain them, and when it does the law is powerless; the governor is powerless, the courts are powerless." McClure went on to say that the Arkansas Republican party could never win so long as whites regarded it as the party of blacks. He implied that white Republicans must perhaps support the elimination of black voting. "I want to see the Negro have all the rights the law gives him, but I am not disposed to cling to him at the expense of party success."[8]

Democrats welcomed a carpetbagger's consent to the sacrifice of black rights, especially now that Democrats were encountering stiff opposition from the militant farmer coalition with blacks and Republicans—the Union Labor ticket—which took 46 percent of the state vote in the 1888 governor's race. The time seemed right to Democrats for disfranchising blacks. Across the South voting restrictions were openly discussed while the North seemed little inclined to resist. In the next campaign the state Democratic party promised both voting restrictions and an end to social equality on railroad cars. The Democratic legislature enacted the new discrimination in 1891, racially separating railroad passengers and requiring a poll tax and a secret ballot for voting. More than half of black voters were eliminated, ending all black political power. After 1894 no black served in either state or local government. Reduced to places within the state Republican party and the federal patronage system, blacks found even these prestige positions under attack as their power waned.[9]

Black leadership protested the loss of power but then conservative leaders, especially ministers, stepped forward to say that despite the unfairness of the new legislation, blacks should turn their attention from protest. As AME Bishop William B. Derrick said:

> You are at the mercy of the American people, they are the power in this country and you had just as well try to make friends with them. You can talk all you want about commanding and demanding things, but that is not the way to get along. You are in a position where you must be humble, and the man who makes his blood and thunder speeches simply plans for the destruction of his own race.[10]

Arkansas' most distinguished black Baptist pastor, E.C. Morris, also recommended that his people turn from protest to economic self-help. The Georgia-born Morris had come to Helena in 1877 as part of the exodus to Kansas. He liked Arkansas and stayed on to build a church, become president of the Arkansas Baptist Convention in 1882, and then the highest position in black Baptist America, president of the National Baptist Convention in 1896. In state politics he took an active role in Republican affairs, serving as a delegate to all state conventions and to three national conventions. Yet Morris advised:

> We have reached the place in our history where we must get out and do something and not stand around complaining about the Negro and his treatment in this country. There is no need of any man telling me that the Negro has a hard time in this country, for his condition is just what he makes it. I find that some Negroes have a hard time and it is because they are too lazy to make it otherwise.

Give less attention to politics and more attention to business and the securement of homes and other property. Let every man among us get a home, improve it, and then add to that a good bank account. Go into the unbroken forest, buy forty, sixty or a hundred acres of land, build a house, move into it and stay there until the last dollar of the purchase price has been paid. Never come to town, except on business, and then to sell rather than to buy. Let the politician, the office-seeker and the merchant look for you, instead of you looking for them.[11]

The Reverend Mr. Morris and Bishop Derrick urged accommodating policies to a people who knew that organized black protest and violence turned out badly for the race. Consider the 1891 Lee County cotton pickers strike. Among the Tennessee blacks who crossed the river to pick cotton in the Arkansas bottoms was thirty-year-old Ben Patterson who organized a cotton pickers strike, demanding a dollar-a-hundred rather than the fifty cents offered. For two days strikers persuaded a majority of pickers to quit work. Then they killed a white overseer and burned a gin, bringing in the sheriff and a posse which killed fifteen men, including prisoners, and ruthlessly suppressed the strike. The Lee County strike ended with harsh repression by white authorities as had the earlier Knights of Labor strike in Pulaski County.[12]

These were the worst years of interracial violence in Arkansas and across the South. In 1892 the increasing number of lynchings peaked with twenty men dying in Arkansas at the hands of mob violence. Even on Main Street in Little Rock a black man was lynched that year. When Governor James Eagle ran into the crowd and attempted to stop the lynching he was knocked down and had to be rescued by friends. The following day the *Arkansas Gazette* came close to defending lynching as the working of a higher law.

It is useless to moralize, and to deplore the reign of the mob. Every good citizen would prefer that the law should take its course. . . . But there are times when human passion becomes a law unto itself. There are times when that higher law which discards legal forms, and marches in a straight line to the execution of its awful decrees, supersedes all other tribunals, and, swift and relentless, hurls the thunderbolts of vengeance against its victims. The brute who assaulted little Maggie Doxey yielded his worthless life to this higher law. His crime was the most atrocious of all crimes; and however we may deplore the methods of the mob, who will say he did not deserve his fate?[13]

Whitecapping inflicted another form of violence upon blacks. Where blacks were a racial minority, whites posted intimidating messages: "Get out of white man's country." If the warnings were ignored, gunfire and dynamite followed. Black homesteaders in the eighties were the first victims but in the nineties violence threatened new manufacturing workers in the lumber camps and mill towns. White hostility to blacks living and working in their communities pushed blacks more and more into the bottom lands and the larger towns where they had the protection of greater numbers, white patrons, and more equitable law enforcement.[14]

The Reverend Mr. Morris lamented the murder of so many blacks. Yet rather than make speeches, which he feared would create more hatred and violence, he advised, "trust God." The same God who had liberated four million from slavery would surely hear their prayers again. "God will not allow these things to continue much longer," he said. "A people who build schools and churches as we are doing, and serve God as we are serving him, I am sure that He will not allow them to be mistreated always." Black Methodists agreed. AME Bishop Evan Tyree reminded his people that the God who had destroyed Egyptian armies in the Red Sea could fight their battles too. Blacks should strive to be sober and industrious while keeping the faith that blessings would come.[15]

Amidst the wave of antiblack violence, there were some more sensitive upland whites who frequently denounced mob violence and occasionally arrested the lawbreakers. And interracial friendships did exist. A Scotch-Irish boy in southwest Arkansas could grow up working with a sharecropper's son. When the white boy explained his career plans, Oscar broke down in tears. He could never go away to Hendrix College and become a minister because he was "a nigger." The white boy's heart went out to Oscar "who had as much sense and as much ambition as he had, but to whom, because of conditions beyond his control, the way seemed closed." The white boy went on to become a prominent Methodist minister and to preach racial toleration with conviction at the annual Race Relations Sunday because he had been affected by Oscar's sobs.[16]

The nineties witnessed a slight shift of emphasis among white Democratic opinion makers. Where the *Arkansas Gazette* had been bitterly antiblack, leading the assault on integration and voting rights, after blacks were legislated into inferiority, the *Gazette* paternalistically turned to defend remaining black rights, especially those protecting their persons and property. The *Gazette* became so "appalled and horrified" when four accused murderers were lynched that it printed such a biting editorial that an attorney in Clarendon, where the lynchings occurred, said the editor "ought to be hung."[17]

While the *Gazette* supported the rule of law and the Booker T. Washington emphasis on education, industry, and property-holding for blacks, it clung to the old Democratic myth that reconstruction had been a horrible time of social equality and black domination. The position of the *Gazette* was clearly mirrored in its reaction to the antiblack stage play, *The Clansman,* by Thomas Dixon. When white Little Rock audiences cheered the drama's Ku Klux Klan and hissed its blacks, the *Gazette* said:

> There is enough of the horrible to satisfy the most morbid taste and disgust the normal. At one stage we have a skulking negro peering through a fence at his expected victim, an innocent child—gloating over his prey. The child follows the path he has taken and presently the alarm comes that she is lost. A searching party takes the trail and the signal to the agonized father is to be one shot if found alive and two if found dead. Two shots ring out and next the Clansmen ride forth to vengeance. The next scene shifts to the cave where the Ku Klux meet and, under a hypnotic spell, the black suspect in a horribly realistic manner lives over again the lying in wait, the luring of the child, the spring at his victim, her flight and leap from the cliff to escape his embrace.
>
> This is horrible enough, but the climax of the unseemly in a stage picture is reached when the negro lieutenant governor makes his vile proposal to the daughter of Austin Stoneman (Thad Stevens), places his arms about her and places her in his private office under guard of two negro henchmen. While he asks her father for her hand in marriage, and, arranging for her immediate death if he attempts violence, sends for a negro preacher to perform the ceremony. No playwright has conceived any climax so revolting and atrocious—especially to be presented in a

section of the country in which the Anglo-Saxon most sturdily asserts his pride of race.[18]

The *Gazette* complained that every white Southerner already knew the story of reconstruction. The Ku Klux Klan had once been "absolutely necessary," the paper said, but Southern whites were no longer in any danger of having black heels put on their white necks or of having blacks ask to marry their daughters. Thus the message of the play was no longer relevant and could only produce unnecessary violence.

Most Arkansas politicians agreed with the *Gazette* except for Governor Jeff Davis who so enjoyed appeals to prejudice that he could not resist borrowing the Mississippi-style attack on black education. "Every time you educate a nigger you spoil a good field hand," Davis said. "If you want to spoil a nigger for good, just call him 'professor'." And Davis could openly urge violence as the proper remedy for threats of social equality. "If a buck nigger should offer to escort a young white woman to church," he would tell voters, "her father, if he were a true Southern white man, would kill the brute as he would a mad dog." It was Governor Davis who ended all black influence in the state Democratic primaries by ordering that the primaries bar blacks.[19]

In the face of overpowering prejudice blacks could only protest every new loss, hope for a better day, and take pride in their growing economic position. Blacks did acquire land in Arkansas: twenty-three percent of black farmers were land owners. Almost forty percent of black tenants owned farming equipment and paid cash rent rather than sharecropping. And, of course, there were success stories such as that of Scott Bond who began freedom as a sharecropper on the St. Francis River and by the age of sixty had acquired 4,000 acres of land, five cotton gins, two general stores, a sawmill, and a son with an Oberlin education. Bond bragged of the economic opportunities in Arkansas while speaking to the 1910 New York convention of the National Negro Business League, and urged this Booker T. Washington organization to hold its next annual meeting in Little Rock.[20]

Blacks living in the state capital could boast that they owned 1500 homes, almost enough for half of their families, 115 small businesses, and two colleges—Arkansas Baptist College and Philander Smith. A few sent their sons to Yale and Harvard. Their greatest urban entrepreneur—John E. Bush—had moved up from teaching and clerking in the post office to organizing a benevolent and fraternal order, the Mosaic Templars of America, which spread through twenty-six states, winning recognition for the secretary-treasurer who paid out the insurance benefit across black America. As the principal lieutenant of Booker T. Washington in Arkansas, Bush also held an important Republican patronage plum, U.S. Land Office receiver, in Little Rock from 1898 to 1913.[21] But despite the achievements of Bush and all the other evidence of economic progress in both urban and rural Arkansas, despite the end of political race baiting, in the twentieth century opportunities for blacks surely declined. The best land had already been opened for cotton, land-hungry populations moved elsewhere, and state economic development slowed. The percentage of landless tenants grew. More blacks moved out than moved into Arkansas. For forty years the black population had grown faster than the white. But in 1910 blacks peaked at 30 percent of the population and thereafter declined steadily, falling to 16 percent by 1980.

While blacks had lost all political equality and had not achieved economic independence they were not without hope for the future nor were they unable to talk of progress. As the Reverend E. C. Morris said, they were free men and women.

> Let us turn back 50 years ago, and look at the condition of our people then, and see us later when we were emancipated, homeless, clotheless and many nameless, and then look at us today, free men and women, and in the places where once stood auction blocks for human slaves we find schoolhouses. We should all feel that we have much to be thankful for today and every other day. I have seen the whole because I have lived in the days of slavery and I know what freedom is.[22]

7

The Politics of Poverty

For two decades the triumphant Arkansas Democratic party talked of little but its liberation of the state from Yankee and black rule. Romanticizing the white man's party as a victory for white pride and local self-government kept voter passions aroused and distracted from controversial economic issues until the 1890s. The economic protest of cotton farmers then forced Democratic politicians to recognize the farmers' misery and to endorse the belief that agrarians were victims of colonial exploitation. The new politics of anticapitalism created a new style of campaigning and the state's greatest politician, Jeff Davis.

The dirt farmer had suffered in a cruel and declining market for a generation. The price of cotton, his major crop, had stood at fifteen cents a pound in the early 1870s but dropped to nine cents in the 1880s and to five cents in the nineties. As prices fell below the farmer's actual cost of production, his suspicion grew that economic suffering resulted from exploitation by the capitalists. Everyone knew that the cotton buyers, the railroad men, the merchants, and the lawyers were building magnificent Victorian mansions in Little Rock while the farmer could not afford new clothes. The system seemed manipulated against the southern farmer who paid the highest interest rates in the nation. Even in his own community the farmer seemed to suffer from monopoly capitalism. The crossroads store charged credit prices which were often double the cash price and in rural areas with thin populations the community had no competing furnishing merchant to offer better prices. A farmer usually had no more choice of merchants or cotton gins than he had of railroads or kerosene. Monopoly capitalists and the money power seemed organized to oppress the agricultural masses.[1]

The redeemer Democrats who controlled state politics—the planter-merchants, lawyers, and businessmen—had not shared the farmers' gloomy analysis. Those who prospered in their connections with capitalism understood cotton prices as the result of overproduction in a world market which grew more slowly than southern production. Rather than sharing farmer concerns, Democratic governors were more likely to be celebrating Arkansas progress since the log cabin days. Railroads had continued to lay new track in the 1880s, increasing the state total to nearly 2000 miles. The forests of Arkansas now attracted northern lumber men and provided the raw material for the major local industry turning wood into boxes, barrels, doors, and furniture. Railroads also carried apples from northwest Arkansas into the national market to win acclaim and profit. In Little Rock the economic progress of Arkansas brought a street railway and lighted and paved streets, as well as factories and machine shops. As the state passed the million population mark by 1890 the urban Democrats even began talking about construction of a new state capitol. The old state house was said to stand in the way of progress because it represented the pioneer days of the Bowie knife and the double log cabin. If Arkansas were to keep in step with progress in other states it must construct a new public monument to express Arkansas intelligence and progress.[2] The urbanites were to win the new state house and a prolonged controversy over its construction.

The farmers were much less persuaded about the evidence of progress. After the 1880s began with a disastrous drought followed by an equally damaging flood, farmers across the state began to join together against the capitalist system. In the western Arkansas River valley a Canadian-born machinist who had homesteaded a farm in Johnson County organized his neighbors into the Brothers of Freedom, a fraternal order of farmers which advocated boycotting the capitalistic system by avoiding debt. Brothers were to diversify their crops to create self-sufficiency and escape from cotton mortgages. That same year, 1882, across in east Arkansas, seven Prairie County farmers gathered in an old log schoolhouse to organize their Agricultural Wheel against the crossroads merchant. They knew a mercantile firm which began with nothing twenty-five years before and now owned 18,000 acres of land taken from farmers by foreclosure of farm mortgages. They, too, feared that their property would be taken and they would be turned into economic slaves of monopoly capitalism unless they organized against robbery mortgages. They, too, urged reduction of cotton planting, crop diversification, and cooperative buying from manufacturers. Farmers flocked to the new organizations and the Wheel rolled into the Brothers of Freedom in the west. The two groups, with a membership of more than 40,000, merged. The new Wheel rolled into nearby states and signed up a half million members before it merged into the National Farmers Alliance. While expanding across the farming states, the Wheel became active in Arkansas politics where the Democrats had remained unresponsive to antimonopoly legislation. In 1888 the political arm of the Wheel, the Union Labor party, gave the Democrats a very close election. The one-legged Confederate veteran, C. M. Norwood, came within 15,000 votes of winning the race for governor in an election especially marked by Democratic ballot fraud. Most Arkansans had voted their old Civil War loyalties (Republicans had endorsed Norwood), but perhaps 50,000 farmers had broken with their Democratic party and voted their opposition to monopoly capitalism.[3]

After a second strong agrarian-Republican protest vote in 1890, alarmed Democrats moved to undercut the opposition, disfranchising most of the black voters, and accommodating the new populist issues. Democrats described their disfranchisement legislation as an election reform which would end scandalous vote frauds and the fear of black domination, allowing white voters to divide over the economic issues. Depriving blacks of the ballot by law did, of course, end the Democratic stealing of black votes, and, by largely eliminating race from politics, forced Democrats towards economic issues (such as free silver and railroad regulation), especially because party primary elections were permitting ordinary voters a voice in the selection of candidates. In earlier elections, the old convention system of selecting candidates had permitted county bosses, businessmen, and attorneys to control the party, but by the nineties local primaries were common. Democratic primary candidates spoke the new populist language, keeping the rural voters from moving into the new Populist Party. In 1896 the Democratic gubernatorial candidate was actually selected by direct primary elections in which Daniel Webster Jones, a redeemer Democrat reborn as a Democratic-Populist, carried the county primaries. The Democratic primaries rewarded a new style of politics: the best stump orator, the most abusive critic of Yankee capitalism succeeded, while the conservative representatives of the establishment were rejected.[4]

The demogogic style begun by Dan Jones was perfected by Jeff Davis, the greatest politician in Arkansas history. The large, baby-faced lawyer from Pope County loved to tickle the voters, share their anger, and raise their hopes. He played the game of politics with outrageous liberties with the truth. No man cared more for winning and less for principles than Davis. He opposed the agrarians in the eighties and then took up their ideas in the nineties, he claimed to be a Hard Shell Baptist while drinking to excess, he attacked the railroads while asking for free rides, he denounced the insurance trust while keeping one of their homeowner's policies. He denounced capitalist Chauncey Depew publicly but apologized privately that it was only politics. Davis was simply the best flim-flam man in the business. He could behave scandalously and still win magnificently because no one ever equaled his campaign performance before discontented Arkansas agrarians.

The Davis popularity began in 1899. He was state attorney general and the legislature adopted an antitrust law which he quickly rode to fame by filing criminal suits against the major corporations, charging that Standard Oil, American Tobacco, the cotton seed oil trust, the insurance companies, and virtually every corporation had engaged in a pool or trust conspiracy to fix prices and should therefore be driven from the state. Just as a local community would keep out a man with smallpox so should Arkansas farmers quarantine all trusts who manipulated prices and impoverished farmers. Naturally the Little Rock businessmen objected to isolating the state from the Yankee world of commerce and therefore defeated Davis's legal case before the state supreme court. But Jeff Davis had launched his war against the corporations. He spoke the language of agrarian radicalism in saying to Yankee corporations, "You shall not cross our borders." He identified himself with the suffering country people against the capitalist interests by relating that the urban press had predicted he could win only the votes of "the fellow with patched breeches and one gallus." Davis professed to be the one-gallus candidate against the urban capitalist class. He stood as the virtuous agrarian candidate in the war against the trusts. "I have to win it from every railroad, every bank, two-thirds of the lawyers, and most of the big politicians," he said, "but, if I can get the plain people of the country to help me, God bless you, we can."[5]

In Davis rhetoric the enemies of the people included Little Rock citizens who were tools and lackeys of the capitalist enemy. They were the ones who hissed and booed Jeff when he stood up to corporations. They were the ones who supported building a new state capitol. "While you are bowed down under the burdensome yoke of starvation and taxation," he said, "they are building a million dollar building in Little Rock and taxing you to pay the bills. They say it will cost a million dollars, but I say to you here and now that by the time you are through paying for it with the money wrenched from you by taxation and for which you have shed your very life's blood, it may cost you five million dollars."[6]

Davis had mastered the most basic requirement of a good politician—making the individual feel important. Before and after his speeches he mingled with the crowds, slapping them on the back, learning their names, and making them believe he cared. Rural people believed Davis was one of them who had shared their lifestyle and who would represent them against the trusts and the urban people. He was the kind of politician who could spot homemade socks in a country store and ask "Is that homemade socks? I'll take them all. My feet ain't been warm since I moved to Little Rock because my wife quit knitting my socks when we moved to town." Country people appreciated these folksy gestures which brought honor to their own life-style.[7]

In debate he had no equal. Without inhibition, he could lie outrageously and make the impossible seem probable. He could take personal letters which belonged to the opposing candidate, read them to the public, and embellish the correspondence until the opponent appeared a scoundrel and a charlatan. His quick wit and skillful use of humor, irony, and ridicule deflated opponents before thigh-slapping audiences. He could take a hostile crowd, quickly touch some shared passion, and have them cheering lustily. He carried every county in Arkansas in 1900 except Pulaski, the home of his Little Rock enemies.

The newly elected governor could win the hearts of the voters but not that of the state legislature, which repeatedly refused to pass his antitrust bill. Surely Davis did not really care whether his legislation became law; he delighted in having enemies to campaign against and waged three campaigns against capitalists interests and his legislature for obstructing the antitrust law. Davis apparently sought friction when he obstructed the legislature's work on the new state capitol and their selection of a state prison farm. He went out of his way to unseat a United States senator with his own candidate and to remove from the State Capitol Commission James P. Eagle, a two-term governor, long-time head of the Arkansas Baptists, and soon to be elected president of the Southern Baptist Convention.

The Davis grab for power resulted in legislative impeachment proceedings and expulsion by the Second Baptist Church of Little Rock. Both Davis and Eagle had belonged to the same congregation until Governor Davis fired his fellow Baptist. Friends of Eagle retaliated by bringing before the congregation discipline committee nine instances of the governor's public drunkeness. When Davis refused to appear to answer the charges, the congregation moved, with only five negative votes, to obey II Thessalonians 3:6, "Now we command you brethren, in the name of our Lord Jesus Christ, that ye withdraw yourselves from every brother that walketh disorderly." Withdrawal of Baptist fellowship would surely have ruined any other politician, but Jeff Davis could turn the disgrace into an asset, saying: "I was expelled from the Second Baptist Church in Little Rock. A lot of high-combed roosters down there, Judge Wood among the members, turned me out of the church for political purposes without a trial, without a hearing, thinking they could ruin me in that way; but when the little church at Russellville, where

I was raised, heard of this indignity, this outrage, they sent for me to come home and join the church of which I had been a member for twenty years, and more than a hundred members were present when I was restored." So in Davis's explanation he had been re-jected not by his denomination but only by big city capitalists. And he could even joke about Baptists and booze, saying that he was only a "pint" Baptist turned out of the church by hypocritical "quart" Baptists.[8]

Davis exploited the weak authority of his Southern Baptist de-nomination where power to judge the sins of a member, hire a min-ister, or even formulate a church creed resided in the individual congregation. This decentralized Baptist democracy left church ministers virtually powerless and inclined to avoid controversial so-cial issues by sanctifying the existing secular order. In Arkansas, as elsewhere across the South, the Southern Baptist faith had become the major regional religion. Stressing personal salvation and the sanctity of the southern way of life, Baptists had overtaken their rivals in every Dixie state except Louisiana. Arkansas Baptists had quickly overtaken the Methodists after the Civil War. Church sta-tistics show that blacks went over to the Baptist religion in larger percentages and greater numbers than whites; yet, among whites, Baptist membership now equaled or exceeded that of Methodists who were governed by a church hierarchy a little more critical of the status quo, more supportive of the social gospel, and affiliated with the Northern Federal Council of Churches. Thirteen percent of white and seventy-two percent of black Arkansas Methodists were members of northern branches of the faith. The major Methodist Episcopal Church South would, in 1939, reunite with the northern denomination; but no Arkansas Baptists affiliated with the North-ern Baptist Convention and neither would their Southern Baptist Convention ever reunite with the Northern Convention.[9] Local Baptists were simply more Arkansan, more southern, and surely more likely to support Jeff Davis.

Though the prohibitionists detested Davis, the voters loved him despite or perhaps even for his vices. Davis often extended mercy to other sinners and lawbreakers. He freely issued pardons for con-'victs and virtually promised the voters that he would pardon any of their relatives who were sentenced to the state penitentiary. He said:

> Do not criticize, my fellow citizens, an executive for exercising mercy. I have a little boy at home eight years old, God bless his little soul! If he should get into trouble in after years and get into the penitentiary, I would kiss the very feet of the governor who would give him a pardon. I would wash his feet with my tears. If it were your son or your brother or your father I could not write the pardon quick enough. Judge Wood said the other day in one of his speeches that any old woman could get a pardon at my office who came in crying. I want to say to you, my fellow citizens, that I thank God that my heart has not become so stilled, so cold and callous that the tears of mothers in Israel will not move me to pity, and when I get this way I want God to take me not only out of the governor's office, but off this earth of ours. . . . If you don't want your boys pardoned, don't come crying around my office, because I cannot stand it, and do not try to stand it.[10]

Success made Davis more and more a comic figure. He began to campaign from an oxcart and call his country audience "rednecks" and "hillbillies." To the disgust of those middle-class urban Arkansans who sought to escape the state's backward image, Davis seemed a character straight out of the *Arkansas Traveler* or the humor of Opie Read. "If you red-necks or hill-billies ever come to Little Rock be sure and come to see me—come to my house. Don't go to the hotels or the wagon-yards, but come to my house and make it your home while you are in the capital city. If I am not at home tell my wife who you are; tell her you are my friend and that you belong to the sun-burned sons of toil. Tell her to give you some hog jowl and turnip greens. She may be busy making soap, but that will be all right; you will be properly cared for, and it will save you a hotel bill."[11] A milk cow may have grazed on the executive lawn during an election campaign but no lye soap or tourists were ever taken on by the Davis family.

Davis moved easily from humor to demagoguery, appealing to prejudices as freely as to any other emotion in the drive to win applause and votes. When Booker T. Washington dined at the White House with President Theodore Roosevelt, Davis pretended outrage at the threat of "nigger equality." "I say that nigger domination will never prevail in this country, that it will never prevail in the beautiful Southland of ours, as long as shotguns and rifles lie around loose and we are able to pull the trigger."[12] He had been too young for service in the Confederacy but compensated by wearing a suit of Confederate grey and denouncing Republicans more furiously than anyone else. He told his audiences that "you might scrape hell with a fine-tooth comb" and you would not find greater fiends than Roosevelt or Arkansas's Powell Clayton "that old one-armed villain, murderer and robber." Republicans, he said, had "robbed our state treasury, they destroyed our schools, they murdered our citizens, they confiscated our property." And the baldest lie of all was that Clayton had murdered Davis's own aunt.

Perhaps Davis's best political maneuver was the tax reduction which he promised when he campaigned for an unprecedented third term. He had guarded the state money so well, he said, that the state was free of debt and taxes might be reduced by half or at least a third. The governor's bookkeeping was as erroneous as his belief that Arkansas schools, which were open only four months a year, were "almost perfect" and needed no more money. At a time when the state offered no support for high schools and remained more than a million dollars in debt, Davis pushed through a tax cut which was great politics but faulty economics.

While progressives accepted the modern capitalist system and sought to regulate it, Davis took the more archaic populist position that the people could destroy the corporations. To rural Arkansans who had shared few of the benefits, ritualistic denunciations of Yankee capitalism were regarded as positive leadership. To be sure, his opposition to the inevitable failed. Although he pushed through his antitrust legislation during the third term and forced some corporations out of Arkansas, a company such as International Harvester or Metropolitan Life only retreated to Memphis and continued to sell to Arkansas customers from the state of Tennessee. A year later, the legislature altered Davis's law and reopened Arkansas to Yankee corporations. By then he had moved on to the United States Senate where he made an occasional antitrust speech for the folks back in Arkansas but was infrequent in voting or attendance.[13]

With Davis retired to the Senate, Arkansans ignored his wishes and elected progressive governors. Most of the rural anger had vanished as farm prices rose after 1900 to the profitable levels of the 1870s. The old rail fence began to disappear as prosperous farmers bought wire fences. By 1915 the *Gazette* could report the demise of the razorback hog, the log cabin, and the coonskin farmer. A journalist who spent three weeks in remote upland communities of Hempstead County reported that the typical farmer now subscribed to a weekly paper and a farm journal, talked intelligently of scientific farming, and owned an impressive array of mule-drawn equipment—harrows, planters, disks, mowers, and rakes. The farmer's wife lived in a painted frame house with flowers in front and a smokehouse, henhouse, and vegetable garden behind. A hillbilly or a redneck could still be found in Arkansas but they were a vanishing type. Even in the Ozark highlands, where settlers clung to the frontier style of life, capitalism touched the lives of the residents during the progressive period. In remote Newton County, where no railroad ever ran, buyers from Eagle Pencil Company came to harvest the cedar along the Buffalo River and float it down to the North Arkansas Railroad which had been constructed across the Ozarks. Although the railroad never made money, hillbillies found winter employment in timber work, especially cutting railroad ties. A man with a cross-cut saw, a double-bitted ax, a broadax, and wedges could daily hew twelve to twenty railroad ties of white oak which resisted rot for years even though untreated by chemicals. An estimated million ties a year came out of the Ozark hills and made tie-hacking the most common occupation next to farming.[14]

The lumber business buzzed even more in the fertile lowlands where northern capital invested heavily in the 1890s. With two-thirds of the state still in forest, Arkansas quickly moved to fourth largest producer of lumber in the United States. In the peak year of 1907 the industry produced two billion board feet. Prices for timber lands that sold for one dollar an acre in the nineties went to ten dollars as corporations bought tracts of 100,000 acres, built their own railroads, and employed 35,000 wage earners. Arkansas workers were now awakened by the blast of steam whistles and could regulate their day by the early 6:30 shriek followed by blasts at eight, twelve, one, and five o'clock. When the sawmill whistles were

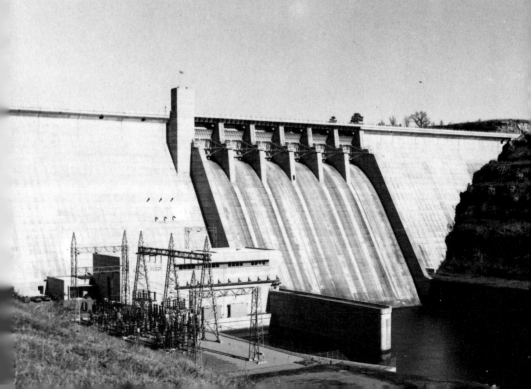

the orthodox Socialist Party of Arkansas no more than eight percent of the state vote. Arkansans had resumed the struggle to join
rather than fight the economic interests of the nation. Surely the
earlier years of poverty politics in Arkansas demonstrates the truth
that in times of crisis or suffering "native common sense provides
no adequate defense against a dedicated fanatic or a wily charlatan
who sets out to play upon the emotions of his fellows."[18] State voters
had repeatedly elected a demagogue who played on their emotions
for his own political purposes and whose rhetoric did more to in-
hibit than to promote radical change. The benefits coming from
the Davis politics were like those of any quack—whether tribal witch
doctor or psychological therapist—who makes the patient feel better without increasing his understanding or altering his social and
economic position.

8

Ruined Again

For the third time in less than a century Arkansas gambled on a scheme to borrow and promote herself into prosperity. The new generation of leaders caught the fever of economic growth, ignored the errors of their fathers, and rode once again the cycle of boom and bust, ending in bankruptcy and defaulting on debts, a record unmatched by any other American state. Others to be sure, had ridden the cycle twice but only Arkansas failed three times, becoming the textbook example of fiscal embarrassment and financial irresponsibility.[1]

Arkansas gullability grew from an excess of optimism that the negative state image of backwardness might finally be erased. Arkansans were increasingly indignant at the hillbilly caricatures which continued the old *Arkansas Traveler* stereotype in the national media. It surely must have been galling to have other Americans think your state a joke, as indeed Arkansas was regarded. When Charles Brough moved to the Chautauqua lecture circuit in 1921 he always drew laughter on being introduced as the former governor of Arkansas. People in other states did think Arkansas laughable.[2]

Quaint rural types, out of step with the modern world, have always been stock figures of comedy for city people. Yet this was especially true in the 1920s when urban America was wresting political control from rural America. Arkansas represented precisely what urban, industrialized people opposed—a rural preindustrial society. City people, distressed about rising food prices as well as rural politics and rural culture, wanted to make farmers in Arkansas and elsewhere more efficient and modern. Agriculture retained the inefficient family farm which produced not only cash crops but much of what the family consumed as well. The variety and number of tasks and small investment in machinery made the farm less efficient than the modern industrial factory. So urban people, seeking cheaper food, began a campaign to make farmers more productive and efficient, to make agriculture like industry. The campaign began with Theodore Roosevelt's Country Life Movement in 1907 and continued with bankers, railroads, and chambers of commerce, seed, fertilizer, and implement companies pushing to sell farmers their services and twentieth century standards of productive efficiency. While urban business pushed its technology the mass media merchandized urban culture and ridiculed rural religion, schools, and politics.[3] In making the rural style odious, the urban press could not resist making Arkansas, the most rural of states, a laughing stock.

The Arkansas leadership—the press, the business community and the politicians from the towns—were outraged by northern urban slanders. They denied the validity of the backward image and pushed their own propaganda about the "Wonder State." But they must have admitted to themselves that the backward image was not entirely false because these same spokesmen worked feverishly to bring their state more rapidly into the modern world by promoting industry, education, and roads while opposing ignorance, the backward-looking Ku Klux Klan, and antievolution laws.[4]

Unable to deny that virtually all Arkansans were rural farmers, the boosters boasted not of their people but of their natural resources. Arkansas was touted as the "Wonder State" of undeveloped resources ranging from diamonds to oil. The state did contain the only diamond mine in North America. Its open pit bauxite mines produced 92 percent of the American aluminum ore. And the 1921 oil rush in El Dorado drilled and pumped enough oil to make Arkansas the sixth leading producer in America. She had all the fossil fuels—oil, gas, coal—and produced electricity too. A homegrown farm boy, Harvey Couch, had turned into an electrical promoter in 1921, after first earning a fortune by building and selling his telephone system to AT&T. He then acquired local electrical generators, tied them together in a system, and sold Arkansas Power and Light securities on Wall Street to construct a major hydroelectric dam on the Ouachita River. By 1925 Couch's system brought the electric age to one-third of the state as well as to parts of Louisiana and Mississippi.[5]

To carry the Wonder State story to America, state boosters created an Arkansas Advancement Association and hired the greatest booster of all—ex-professor and ex-governor Charles H. Brough. This master of inflated eloquence, who could say with a straight face that Arkansas was the only state mentioned in the Bible (Noah looked out of the Ark-and-Saw), received $14,000 a year to join the chautauqua and the lyceum lecture circuits to spread the truth about Arkansas. His official orations were on such subjects as "The Glory of the Old South and the Greatness of the New" but he always took advantage of laughter at his introduction as the "ex-governor of Arkansas" to slip in ten minutes of propaganda about the state. A Brough lecture was a master performance and won applause as the most popular chautauqua speech on the 1922 tour. In addition to the Brough oration, the Arkansas Advancement Association also sent out a million copies of "Three Hundred Reasons Why We are Proud of Arkansas." The group also hired a special railroad train to tour the North, showing Arkansas products, rice queens, and political orators. And in 1923, the state legislature endorsed their approach, dropping the old state nickname "The Bear State" for the more marketable "The Wonder State."[6]

While telling outsiders of the wonderland, state boosters told natives that they must change, they must modernize, they must industrialize. A Profitable Farming Bureau of city bankers and businessmen urged farmers to diversify their crops and then spend more money in town for tractors and other supplies. In 1919 the bureau hired a full-time agricultural orator from Memphis, H. M. Cottrell, to spread the gospel of modern scientific farming, including some very poor advice such as feeding hogs sweet potatoes instead of corn. The bureau also replaced the mules at the agricultural colleges with tractors and predicted that Arkansas farmers would visit their implement dealers and motorize their farms within five years. The Bureau predictions were much too optimistic, but the trend to tractors had definitely begun in 1919, led by Arkansas County where the rice farmers owned 500 tractors. The tractor demanded larger farms, forcing a consolidation of smaller units and decreasing by 10,000 the number of farms in the state by 1925. The increased efficiency of the motorized farms, and lower crop prices, forced economically marginal people from the countryside. One-third of the Arkansas counties lost population by 1925.[7]

Arkansas farmers were quicker to buy the motorized Ford automobile than the tractor. Beginning in the fall of 1916, when cotton prices zoomed upward, farmers, including black sharecroppers, began to buy Fords. The automobile caught the countryman's imagination and made him responsive to the good roads propaganda of auto salesmen and urban centers. Arkansas's routes for land travel were much the same as they had always been, unimproved dirt roads for horseback or wagon travel, deeply rutted and reliable only in dry weather. Even the old military roads across Arkansas had changed little in eighty years. The tree stumps in the roadway were rotted, it was true, and even the original pioneer log houses along the way were now gone except for those fallen stone chimneys, but the road itself remained little changed. Moving west from Memphis towards Little Rock, the old way was "an ordinary, low country road" not even graded until Forrest City. Once in hilly country the old military road had been changed only by erosion which cut the path deeper into the hillsides. This road and all other roads were under local control. There were no state or federal highway numbers because neither branch of outside government had taken over road maintainance. Dangerous gullies and mud holes in the roadway were filled in by local citizens. If a stream could not be forded at low water by a wagon, then it had been proper to ask the state to charter a private ferry or bridge company to accommodate the public and extract a toll from every traveler.[8]

The improvement of roads began in Pulaski County where planters outside the capital city decided to build a gravel road in 1909. The cotton planters between Scott's Station and Eagle used their own men and teams to erect a graded roadbed. The county government built the concrete bridges and contributed $2000 a mile for crushed rock to finish the fourteen mile Scott's Station Pike, a marvelous new road on the way from Little Rock to Pine Bluff. Planters further along the way would organize their own road improvement districts to complete the Pike to Pine Bluff. By 1915 perhaps a hundred miles of the state's roads had been improved. For the other thousands of miles of dirt road, it was a step forward if they were even smoothed occasionally by a split-log drag pulled over the surface to fill in the ruts. "We are sadly lacking in good roads, one of the most essential elements in material prosperity," Governor Brough admitted, "and upon material prosperity depends the intellectual, moral and cultural greatness of the state."[9]

The automobile and the highway captured the imagination of rural Arkansas in the flush times of forty-cent cotton during the First World War. But the costs of improved roads were enormous. The first grading of a wagon path cost $5000 a mile, clearly more than local government could afford. The state constitution prohibited county government from borrowing for public improvements, placing an intolerable barrier against progress and forcing residents to organize a new division of local government. New auto owners solved their road financing problem by imitating the swampland developers of east Arkansas who created drainage districts with taxing authority to sell bonds, dig canals to reclaim the wetlands, and then tax the landowners to repay the bond debt. The possibilities of the taxing district scheme quickly resulted in more than two hundred road improvement districts and a frenzy of bond selling and road building.[9]

Road construction initially pleased both motorists and farmers. Where a cotton wagon in the muddy ruts of Faulkner County had required a six-mule team and an entire day to deliver its bale to the railroad station six miles away, the trip on a new gravel road took less than two hours even with an increased load of six bales and a much smaller two-mule team. Crops now rushed to market and a motor bus delivered children to school even on rainy days. This was indeed progress.[10]

Then came the postwar depression and the collapse of cotton prices. Farmers feared the road taxes would force them into bankruptcy. By the spring of 1921 the *New York Times* reported "Arkansas Totters Under Road Taxes." Farmers threatened violence against road improvement leaders. Guns and organized intimidation forced road commissioners in Craighead County to resign. Governor Thomas McRae echoed the farmers' dismay, "this road business," he said, "has turned out to be the greatest disaster that has ever befallen the people of Arkansas."[11] By fall, however, after cotton prices partially recovered, much of the local criticism of road building also disappeared.

Criticism of the local road system continued from the state boosters who objected that localism could never build a state highway system. The local people wanted roads from their farm to the railroad station and were not ready for tourist roads. "We don't care about roads going to Chicago, New Orleans or St. Louis," one had said. "We are interested in roads from our farms to railway stations—to get our children to school and products to market—that is what we have been doing."

The old local system did have powerful supporters. Local road building put money and patronage in the hands of local leaders. Naturally the commissioners of the improvement districts and the county judges, who handled the money for upkeep of local roads, opposed state intervention. They wanted control of the tax revenues, even those the state collected for auto registration and gasoline. The local forces were so powerful that only federal intervention broke their monopoly on roads. The federal government cut off financial aid for Arkansas roads in 1923 until the state assumed control of major highways and approved a four-cent-a-gallon gasoline tax for building the highway system.

Under the new 1923 Harrelson law the main highways were more uniformly graded and graveled, the larger streams bridged, and even some concrete paving begun. Yet travel remained uncertain and reading the newspaper road report continued to be essential for a motorist. Every wet season some gravel roads turned to mud. Even the newly numbered U.S. Highway 64 became impassable in the Mulberry River bottoms of western Arkansas and in the White River bottoms of eastern Arkansas. Impatience to complete the highway system and continued local opposition to paying the heavy property taxes for road district bonds brought a new departure in financing and road building in 1927.[12]

In this new age of the motor vehicle, prevailing wisdom said that Arkansas suffered as great an economic and social handicap without a modern system of trunk roads as she had suffered in the earlier years without a railroad system. "The automobile has completely changed the old order of things," governor-elect John E. Martineau said. "Arkansas will progress only as her road system progresses."[13] The *Arkansas Gazette* agreed that building roads improved the state while bad roads retarded development. "The traditional backwardness of some mountain counties"the *Gazette* said, "must be traced . . . to their inaccessability which imposes on these localities many of the conditions of pioneer life." Bad roads held back the development of farming and industry as well as education and even religion. Bad roads, the *Gazette* concluded, "retarded development spiritually as well as economically."[14]

The *Gazette* was speaking the language of southern liberalism, a creed well expressed by Arkansas-born Edwin Mims' *The Advancing South* (1926). This book of essays explained the war of liberation against "the conservatism, the sensitiveness to criticism, the lack of freedom that have too long impeded Southern progress." Poverty and ignorance in the South were on the defensive as younger college men "freer of traditions and prejudice"took up the battle against religious fundamentalism, antievolution, and the Klan, moving the South towards the freedom of the modern world. The intellectual and industrial developments underway in the South created a "land of opportunity"for the intellectual and spiritual emancipation of a section.[15]

If poor roads retarded the development of Arkansas, then the construction of modern highways should be speeded up. All public leaders were optimists and state boosters. All agreed that the state should spend much more aggressively. As the number of automobiles had grown dramatically from 60,000 to 210,000 in the first six years of the twenties, so had state revenues from the auto registration and gasoline tax, making the state financially able to spend more. And the state could also borrow money. The years without credit or lenders had ended when New York bankers were persuaded by Governor Brough in 1917 to make short-term loans. During the following decade the state had built a better credit rating which state leaders now wanted to use for speeding up highway construction and for taking over the local district debts. So Gov. John E. Martineau's administration assumed the $50 million debt of the local road districts, relieving landowners of local road taxes, and prepared to borrow an additional $1 million a year for highway and bridge construction.[16]

Arkansas leadership could not be faulted for its original Martineau road law, but the politicians quickly became intoxicated on easy bond money. The legislature borrowed $3 million a year to provide Confederate veterans and their widows the finest pension in the South, $50 a month. And the highway borrowing accelerated so rapidly that the state acquired a highway and bridge debt of $150 million in 1932. To be sure, Arkansas could offer excuses, such as the disastrous 1927 flood which ruined many a road and bridge, to justify additional borrowing. But the truth was that Arkansas's political leaders, led by Gov. Harvey Parnell, were hooked on borrowed money and continued selling bonds until their credit entirely collapsed. "We have mortgaged the future for two generations to come," the *Gazette* admitted. "Babies now in their cradles will have grown children of their own before the borrowed money we have spent on highways is repaid."[17]

Despite all the borrowing, the state had finished only half the highway system. According to the Official Arkansas Highway Map of 1930 a Little Rock motorist could drive only to Hot Springs, Conway, or Lonoke on a paved road. No concrete or asphalt highway had been completed across the state. The U.S. highways which ran through Arkansas were largely gravel but even some ungraveled dirt remained, such as Highway 70 west of Memphis. U.S. Highway 64 between Clarksville and Mulberry remained unfinished with sections of ungraveled dirt. Local roads could be much worse. On the official map "unimproved earth" was not even the poorest type of road; "impassable" denoted the worst local roads.

Some scapegoat, some villain had to be identified. An audit of the state highway commission records began, driving an engineer and a road contractor to suicide and reporting "shocking extravagance and waste." In repentance for having supported such reckless spending, the voters turned to a white-haired Jeffersonian, J.M. Futrell, who assured them that the only solution for financial extravagance and the onset of the nation's worst depression was a reduction of state government by half and a return to the least and best government. In addition, the state legislature should be restrained by an amendment stripping it of the power to issue bonds without voter approval.[18]

The total Arkansas debt of $160 million seems small in modern dollars but it was then the fourth largest state debt, placing Arkansas behind only New York, Illinois, and Louisiana. With a smaller population and much smaller financial resources, Arkansas had acquired the heaviest debt of all. As her per capita income shrank to $212 during the thirties, her state debt of $75 for every man, woman, and child became even heavier. Arkansas defaulted on interest payments in 1932, becoming the only state to fail to pay its bonded obligations during the Great Depression.

Arkansas would long suffer from her borrowing excesses of the twenties. The citizens did not wish to accept the odium of living in the only American state to repudiate its debts, but neither could they pay. Politicians sought to scale down the interest rates and stretch out the payments but bond holders indignantly objected. So almost a decade passed before the state could resolve the issue by turning to the federal government for low interest loans to repay its creditors.[19]

9

Driving out the Arkies

The old agricultural economy collapsed during the 1930s, creating thousands of refugees from traditional rural life. Within a single generation, two-thirds of the state's farmers were eliminated, becoming part of the southern farm population of seven million forced from the land by the 1960s. These were the years in which 850,000 Arkansans, to escape the deprivations of rural poverty, fled north or west to the cities of America. The story of driving off more than forty percent of the state's population, of uprooting and migration, dominated the lives not only of those who left but also of those who remained behind.

The moving force in the destruction of the old society was the industrialization of agriculture. Just as the nineteenth century had witnessed the introduction of machinery and the organization of manufacturing on a large scale, so did the twentieth see farming made more productive by eliminating workers. Each tractor replaced nine men and mules. Each mechanical cotton picker did the work of one hundred field hands. But many inefficient farmers continued their ruinous competition until by the sixties machinery and chemical herbicides had eliminated stoop labor and two-thirds of the farmers. In retrospect, the outcome seemed so certain that a modern historian puzzles over the resistance to change; yet thousands of those involved in the process endured much misery and strugged desperately against the inevitable.[1]

The first cries of distress arose after the terrible summer of 1930. Hot cloudless days with temperatures rising to 110 degrees and the driest season on record ruined both field crops and gardens. The drought, accompanied by economic depression and the failure of local banks, brought hunger to Arkansas that winter. So desperate were white farmers around England, Arkansas, on January 3, 1931, that they threatened violence when the Red Cross ran out of order blanks for food rations. "Our children want food and we are going to get it!" a crowd of forty shouted as they marched on local merchants who agreed to issue food without Red Cross order blanks. Across the state at least three similar raids occurred but went unreported by the local press and politicians who sought to prevent further panic.[2]

Only the Red Cross and a bumper fall crop of turnips saved Arkansans from starvation. In those terrible times a rural bard, Joe Page, put the tragedy and salvation to rhyme.

> We didn't have any dollars
> And hardly any dimes,
> When the neighbors met up
> They talked about hard times.
>
> The cotton all burned up
> And the corn was in the shock
> And it began to thunder
> And rain began to drop.
>
> The thunder it got louder,
> It was a sight to see it rain,
> We raised lots of turnips
> And a patch of sorghum cane.[3]

A much better growing season for the 1931 crops failed to bring prosperity to farmers who were forced to sell their cotton for five cents a pound. Prices refused to rise until the New Deal plowed under one-third of the cotton crop in 1933. The reduction in acreage did move prices up a few cents, helping planters survive, while injuring a third of the sharecroppers whose labor was no longer needed. To protect themselves from evictions and to secure their share of the government payments for crop reductions, share-croppers in east Arkansas organized a union in the summer of 1934. The biracial Southern Tenant Farmers Union spread through the delta counties of Craighead, Poinsett, Cross, Crittenden, and Mississippi where the plantations of lumber companies sometimes ran up to 25,000 acres. In the economic contest between the share-croppers and the landlords, American socialists intervened on the side of the little people, bringing down the wrath of the planter establishment.[4]

When the leader of the American Socialist party, Norman Thomas, stepped up on the porch of a black church in Birdsong to speak before the assembled sharecroppers in March of 1935 he was shoved aside by a planter who said: "There ain't goin' to be no speaking here. We are citizens of this county and we run it to suit ourselves. We don't need no Gawd-damn Yankee Bastard to tell us what to do with our niggers." Freedom of speech and assembly disappeared as meetings were banned and armed vigilantes patrolled the highways beating and murdering union organizers. The union officials fled to Memphis, Tennessee, and Norman Thomas reported to the nation: "There is a reign of terror in the cotton country of eastern Arkansas. . . . The plantation system involves the most stark serfdom and exploitation that is left in the western world."[5]

Reports of planter ruthlessness and exploitation misled New Deal intellectuals into believing that landlords were the problem. The New Deal solution attempted to turn sharecroppers into independent small farmers. At the resettlement communities of Dyess, Lakeview, Plum Bayou, and Lake Dick former tenants were placed in white frame houses with red barns, twenty to forty acres of land, and a $6,000 mortgage. At the same time small farmers were being displaced by the tractor and mechanized farming, the federal resettlement projects sought to establish a higher standard of living than small farms could ever support. Payments on the mortgages could never be made from the earnings on twenty acres and so inevitably the farms were abandoned and the projects failed.[6]

For a small farmer to survive required the industry and hustle of a Dolan Burris of the upland Buttermilk Valley who supplemented his farm income by teaching in the local one-room school. Without a college education, he had passed the teachers exam and taught in the short winter rural school term. After school he milked his cows and then grabbed a tow sack, called his hunting dog, and pursued fur bearing opossums into the night. On Saturdays he drove into Atkins to buy furs from other farmers for resale in the fur market. When the school session ended he farmed, baled hay, picked cotton, and worked in a rock quarry. His autobiography describes his life as one of "hard work and hardships."[7]

The life of the farm wife, Burris reported, was equally hard. Without electricity or running water the weekly washday was indeed blue Monday with water to draw from the well and carry to the cast iron washpot where a wood fire had been built to heat the water and boil the clothes. Dirt was forced from the clothes by rubbing each item on a rub-board in a tub of hot soapy water. The clothes were then rinsed and wrung out by hand and hung on the line to dry. A flat iron heated on the inside wood cookstove removed the wrinkles. The rural Arkansas woman's work with clothing and food was an endless cycle.

Agriculture provided a poor living even for the larger planters. The 1934 average income for thousand-acre plantations figured out to $2,528. If six percent interest on the planter's $31,378 capital investment were subtracted, then he was left with only $645.32 for his year's work. Even in a better year, 1937, that wage climbed to only $1,339.76. Clearly no bloated capitalist, the average planter earned modest profits. For those who sought to increase their earnings, greater productivity required reducing the number of tenants. Plowing could now be done by tractors but hand labor could not be eliminated from cotton chopping and picking which were yet to be mechanized. Only by hiring wage workers could tenants be replaced. Around population centers, where workers could be hired off street corners at 4 A.M., tenants began to be replaced. But 80% of the delta farms continued with tenants into the forties.[8]

The tenant union inevitably failed to survive or to raise the income of its people. All the army of writers who discovered the Arkansas sharecropper and jouneyed to the delta to aid the disinherited in their struggle could never change the economic system. The only choice for liberation came from migration, but this was especially difficult during the depressed thirties when urban areas were unable to find employment even for their own residents.

More than 128,000 Arkansans did leave the state during the thirties, but that was fewer than in the twenties when urban prosperity permitted Arkansans to establish more significant contacts with the North and West. In east Arkansas thousands of blacks had moved north. By 1930, 5000 Arkansas blacks had moved to Memphis, 10,000 to St. Louis, and 12,000 to Chicago. In Detroit and every major midwestern city, Arkansas-born blacks were counted by the census of 1930.[9] The patterns of out-migration had been established by those who had already moved on. When urban jobs became available those left behind were certain to hear through family or friends and rush to join the ranks of the out-migrants.

White Arkansans, too, had their outside contacts. Everybody in east Arkansas seemed to know someone in Michigan. Farther west in the poor hill country where white tenant farmers averaged $134.71 per year, the migration patterns were to Texas or California. Hill-country cotton farmers sold out in hopes that the better lands of west Texas would improve their fortunes. Thirty-six thousand Arkies went on to California to become part of the army of migrant farm refugees who replaced Mexican workers in the thirties and dramatized rural poverty. The Oklahoma refugees were more numerous and received the bulk of literary attention in the press and in John Steinbeck's *The Grapes of Wrath* (1939), but Arkies were there, too, in the San Joaquin Valley. In 1934, for example, three young men from the northwest county of Carroll drove a Ford to California and then returned boasting of having earned $150 apiece as migratory workers. A Carroll County exodus followed, creating a Little Arkansas of 200 residents on the outskirts of Greenfield, California.[10]

A few hillcountry Arkansans had been moving to the land of oranges ever since the 1849 gold rush. But only after the automobile became a common possession did families drive west and then return to report on the promised land. In 1926, for example, Earnest Worley of the Ozark mountains bought a T-model half-ton truck, stretched canvas over the back, and started for California with his family in the modern covered wagon. The trip then took a month and averaged two flat tires a day. Once in California, where the Worley children were required to attend school, the mountain people knew the state was no place for them and returned to the hills of Arkansas.[11]

The hard times of the thirties, however, drove thousands of Arkansans to reconsider their local attachments. They lacked not only the income for obtaining basic necessities but also all the modern conveniences. The upland farmers lacked electricity. Not even two percent of Arkansas farms had electric power and the private power companies had no interest in extending their lines into rural areas, claiming that there was no profit in a rural line or farm people couldn't afford electricity.[12] So the farmer's wife had no electric lights, refrigerator, fan, or washing machine. Neither did farm homes have indoor plumbing or telephones. Women especially wanted to have the modern household conveniences and urged their husbands to move when jobs became available.

After America entered the war against Japan and the Axis powers in December 1941 the defense plants, especially in California, created a labor shortage. The shipyards in Oakland provided almost a half million new jobs. If an Arkie could not get a shipyard job at least he could take an unskilled job left by a Californian who took the higher paid defense work. So hillcountry Arkansans by the thousands moved west. Those with cars drove them. If you had no car then you hired a ride from an enterprising truck driver such as Berry Hefley, a timber worker who put in seats and a canvas cover over his log truck and offered rides for $25. He loaded fifty to sixty individuals, drove around the clock for three days, and delivered his load of eager Arkansas workers. Hefley then took a job himself until a group wanted to go home. After returning to Arkansas he recruited another load to take west to California.[13]

During the forties more than eight million American farm people migrated to urban areas. Migration from southern farms surpassed that of other sections and in Arkansas migration exceeded the southern average, with 38.5 percent of the state farm population leaving agriculture. With so few urban areas in the state, most were forced to go outside Arkansas to find work. During the decade 416,117 residents left Arkansas, and in the next decade outmigration was even heavier. So, by 1960 almost 44 percent of the Arkansas population had left. Only the state's continuing high birth rate kept the total population from declining more than 8.5 percent to 1,786,272.[14]

Two-thirds of the Arkansas farms disappeared as the western hill country abandoned cotton and row crop agriculture. In the east the final replacement of the cotton hoe and the picking sack ended tenant farming and most agricultural wage labor. A new two-row cotton picker could do the work of 100 field hands. And the chemical herbicides destroyed weeds and grass without hand labor. Even cotton itself ceased to be the major delta crop as soybeans, which required fewer chemicals and less labor, rose to the top as the number one crop, while cotton fell to sixth place.

The out-migration included not only the agricultural workers but many of the educated and the skilled as well. Like all agricultural states without major urban centers, Arkansas lost its young college graduates. When the University of Arkansas graduates in business administration interviewed for jobs, they were recruited by firms in Houston, Dallas, Kansas City, and Miami, but not Arkansas. A single Texas department store, Foleys in Houston, hired thirty marketing graduates in the 1950s while Little Rock department stores took only two. Graduates in the liberal arts also left for adjoining states at the rate of fifteen for every one who stayed.[15]

The common wisdom of young Arkansans was expressed by a student from a small northeast town who said: "There's nothing for me back home. They are talking about a new factory, but I don't think they will get it. I don't think any college graduates have ever come back to town since I can remember." Another student said: "The seniors who have big ideas and hopes, the ones who imagine themselves rich at thirty, the ones who will be the doers and movers and wheelers and dealers, will leave the state for greener pastures. And I don't blame them."[16]

Those Arkansans who remained suffered a mass inferiority complex unique among the peoples of an American state. Having none of the grandeur of the Old South and little of the wealth of the New, Arkansans needed an explanation, an excuse. In common with other neurotics, they were inclined to lash out with excessive aggressiveness towards critics and especially northerners. The old chip-on-the-shoulder defensiveness of Jeff Davis prevailed among the elite as well as the masses. That local anger against northern capitalists can be found in John Gould Fletcher's *Arkansas* (1947). This privileged son of a Little Rock businessman had lived in Europe, won a Pulitzer Prize for poetry, and yet shared the agrarian distrust of Yankees who were accused of exploiting the state, treating its citizens as a colonial people, and then hypocritically accusing them of mistreating their blacks.[17]

The Arkansan's need for recognition, for some measure of success, brought a fierce pride in any local product which won favorable recognition outside the state. Even John Gould Fletcher could interrupt his agrarian lament to boast of the state's "important" new politician, J. William Fulbright, with whom "Arkansas stepped boldly and vigorously on the stage of international affairs."[18] For three decades Arkansans applauded their native son who won recognition from the nation's intellectual establishment. Although born to commercial wealth in Fayetteville, educated in England on a Rhodes scholarship, and married to a Philadelphia society girl, J. William Fulbright also posed as plain Bill, the University of Arkansas football star turned farmer with a log cabin—Rabbit Foot Lodge. Really a law school professor turned university president, Fulbright entered Congress after partisan governor Homer Adkins fired him in 1941. Fulbright's Oxford education had turned him into a Atlantic intellectual who believed political leadership the greatest challenge of his generation. In Congress he won acclaim for enacting the first wartime resolution to create a United Nations and then his postwar Fulbright student-professor exchange made him internationally famous as an advocate of world peace and greater understanding among nations. As chairman of the Senate Foreign Relations Committee, after 1959, he led a scholarly criticism of American Cold War blunders, culminating in his Vietnam War hearings. Admirably schooled for his dissenting, his outside role, Fulbright had been reared in a Republican family among a people where most grew to adulthood without ever meeting a Republican. Of course, posing as a Democrat was required of any elected official in Arkansas. From the only region in America—the South—which had lost a foreign war, Fulbright shared less of the "arrogance of power" than most American senators. For an educated Arkansan who knew the burden of his state history, the possibility of an American failure rarely seemed absurd. As one who shared the state's resentment of outside exploitation, Fulbright could also understand the Third World resentments of American policies. As the powerful analyst of American diplomacy, Fulbright was often out of step with Arkansas opinion but the voters kept him in office as long as they suffered an inferiority complex because his fame gave them a bit of pride—not a small benefit in Arkansas. As the *Arkansas Democrat* had said in 1944, "Congressman Fulbright, in his first term in Washington, has gained more favorable publicity than any other Representative we have ever sent to Congress."[19]

10

The Faubus Detour

Arkansas emerged from the Second World War with its promoters of progress restored to leadership. And for more than a decade the new generation of boosters reshaped Arkansas in the national image. The Americanization of the state continued until a wily politician detoured back to the archaic Dixie rhetoric, playing to the racial fears and frustrations of many white citizens. The Faubus detour, although only a temporary backsliding from Americanization, dominated an entire generation of state history.

The recovery of faith in progress had begun during World War II with massive doses of federal money pumped through new military installations and war industries, elevating the per capita income from $252 to $654 and ending the depression of the thirties. The federal government constructed two large army training centers, Camp Joe T. Robinson outside Little Rock and Camp Chaffee outside Fort Smith, as well as five air bases, a prisoner-of-war camp, and two Relocation Centers for detention of Japanese-Americans. Half a dozen new munitions factories sprang up across the state and two enormous aluminum processing plants, Hurricane Creek and Jones Mill, were constructed. With federal money financing growth, the industrial revolution finally reached Arkansas.[1]

The wheels of industry turned on electricity provided by Arkansas Power and Light. As the demand for new kilowatts of power increased two and a half times, AP&L's taste for profits grew along with its fears that competing public power, another TVA, might move into Arkansas if the company did not supply the wartime demand for power. So AP&L rushed into the bond market for expansion money and then worried about where to sell its new kilowatts when the war ended. AP&L thus became an Arkansas booster to lure new factories into the state to replace the war industries. In 1944 the president of AP&L, C. Hamilton Moses, launched his new booster program by organizing an Arkansas Economic Council for attracting outside industries. Arkansas communities were urged to make themselves more attractive by building better schools, water works, and sewage systems. Northern industries were propagandized about the merits of moving to Arkansas—low wages and taxes, an eager work force, and a New South state rapidly rising above the old peculiar institutions of Dixie.[2]

The industrial propaganda contained some truth. The state of Arkansas had been growing less southern. The University of Arkansas, located in the northwest, turned in the 1920s to the North Central Association of Colleges and Universities rather than the Southern Association. Northern educated professors were employed and some state legislators even attacked the University in January of 1933, asserting that "foreigners of the rankest kind" and "rank northerners" were installed as faculty members. By the thirties, even the small Conway State Teachers College had Dr. Maude Carmichael, southern-born but Columbia and Radcliffe educated, who taught that environment rather than genetic inheritance explained why blacks lagged behind. A student could begin her course "as racist as anybody" but leave believing that racial segregation in education and elsewhere prevented blacks from having an equal opportunity.[3]

White believers in equal opportunity did exist in Arkansas and in the exaggerated promotional message of industrialist Hamilton Moses, determined to lure northern industry, Arkansas was even said to be ready for an end to Jim Crow. Moses could say that only the older people objected to white and black children going to the same school. "I have talked to many white high-school boys and girls about this, and not one said he or she would mind having Negroes in their classes. But don't quote me."[4]

In truth, liberals were not very outspoken on race in Arkansas politics. Even Brooks Hays, who had opposed the Ku Klux Klan in the twenties and the poll tax in the thirties and who had been one of the handful of political liberals in the South who worked with the Southern Conference on Human Welfare in the 1930s, had never publicly admitted an official connection with the organization nor did he publicly support desegregation. The Brooks Hays who was elected to Congress in 1942 went believing in justice for blacks but also that white fears must be permitted to delay desegregation. Hays had an enlightened Baptist conscience but was also enough of a politician to resist moving beyond the white racial consensus to oppose Jim Crow segregation publicly. He preferred to avoid controversial issues. "If Brooks is as good a two-stepper as he is a side-stepper," one observer said, "I'll bet he's popular at them Little Rock dances."[5]

The postwar debate over race ignited with President Truman's February 2, 1948, civil rights message. Truman endorsed not only antilynching and voting rights legislation but also an end to segregation on interstate transportation. Arkansas at first seemed to turn towards Dixie and continued segregation when its governor, Ben Laney, joined in organizing the Dixiecrat rebellion against Truman; but the Arkansas boosters stepped forward to reject Dixie candidates and remain national Democrats. Arkansans replaced their Dixiecrat governor with a young liberal, Sid McMath, who kept the state within the Democratic party, helping to insure Truman's re-election and gaining a friend in the White House.[6]

The young governor gave Arkansas a glamorous New South symbol. The thirty-six-year-old Marine hero and former prosecuting attorney, who had cleaned up vice and corruption in Hot Springs, led the state towards modernization in both economics and race. He adopted the *Arkansas Gazette's* moderate racial stance that the local legislature ought to enact its own antilynching and antipoll tax legislation to make federal intervention unnecessary. McMath welcomed blacks into the Democratic party and appointed them to formerly all-white commissions. He seemed the industrial developers' ideal governor, pushing through a highway bond issue, ignoring the warnings of the older generation, and paving both highways and farm-to-market roads. He was the best salesman since Brough. When Arthur Godfrey interviewed the governor for his radio show and expressed surprise to find that McMath wore shoes, McMath laughed and replied "Yes, we not only wear shoes, but we manufacture shoes in Arkansas."

A dozen shoe plants had emerged in Arkansas after the Second World War. If the local community would build the plant, then the International Shoe Company of St. Louis would agree to organize a shoe assembly factory. Ambitious regional trade centers, such as the east Arkansas town of Searcy, were eager to gain the 413 new jobs. So Searcy, with a population of 3,000, sold bonds to raise the $110,000 for a factory building and won its first nonlumber industry. The wages were low, 55 cents an hour, but after a decade of steady employment shoe factory workers were building new homes in the town suburbs. A half dozen other companies were also lured into Searcy during the next decade, raising the total of manufacturing wages by 350 percent, which helped to create an additional two service jobs in town for each new manufacturing job. The town grew by twenty percent in population, developed seven new residential districts, and became a model of the new booster community in Arkansas.[7]

Arkansas governors would come and go, but industrial growth remained the New South faith supported by all. A most dramatic success for industrial promotion occurred in 1955 when Gov. Orval Faubus persuaded Winthrop Rockefeller to head the Arkansas Industrial Development Committee. Rockefeller, a grandson of the businessman who formed the first industrial combination in manufacturing—Standard Oil—had recently moved into the state. He had been the nonconformist of the five grandsons, Yale dropout, oil field worker, infantry soldier, and New York playboy. But in 1953 he moved away from a bad marriage to settle down in the Sunbelt and devote his last twenty years to farming, philanthropy, and politics. He built a ranch on Petit Jean Mountain, west of Little Rock, and launched a farming operation that ran to 24,000 acres and extended beyond the state boundaries.[8]

The Rockefeller name attracted attention from the national media, always fascinated by wealth and power, while the family connections assisted Winthrop in recruiting an effective organization. Brother David, the Chase Manhattan banker, helped hire two experienced northern industrial promoters who could effectively package Arkansas assets for national advertising. The Rockefeller name also impressed the state legislature. When Winthrop asserted that better schools were necessary for successful industrial promotion campaigns, state representatives promptly raised the state sales tax to support education.

Hopes for industrial growth seemed so widely shared that none could oppose it. Yet, in 1957, Gov. Orval Faubus was forced to choose between preserving the image of a progressive Arkansas or furthering his own political career. He wanted a third term, a unique political victory which only Jeff Davis had achieved in the entire past history of the state. To get that third term would surely require a detour back to the Dixie rhetoric against Yankee imperialism and social equality.[9] Such a campaign also seemed to require a personal betrayal of his own middle name, Eugene. His father had so believed in the brotherhood of the working class that he named Orval after the socialist leader Eugene Debs and later encouraged him to study at the radical Commonwealth College.

Desegregation in the state had been under way for almost a decade. Arkansas, the first southern state to break the Jim Crow barrier in education, had voluntarily desegregated its university law school in 1948. There the law school dean had forseen the inevitablility of integration and maneuvered to avoid litigation by gaining the consent of the university board and the state governor, Ben Laney. In February of 1948 Dean Robert A. Leflar admitted Silas Hunt to the law school at Fayetteville. During the next decade all the state colleges and five high schools admitted black students. Central High in Little Rock seemed only another peaceful, gradual step in desegregation. The industrious superintendent, Virgil Blossom, had begun working on a plan immediately after the Brown desegregation decision. The Blossom plan for token integration in the fall of 1957 had the support of all six members of the Little Rock school board. White segregationists, however, opposed the plan and so did the local NAACP, led by Daisy Bates. A bitter light-skinned woman whose mother had been raped and killed, presumably by white men, Mrs. Bates felt intensely about discrimination and tokenism, but failed to persuade the federal court to alter the Blossom Plan. So the modest beginnings of desegregation in the state capital with nine black and 1800 white students were scheduled for the fall of 1957.[10]

White resistance, however, was rising as desegregation approached. The White Citizens' Council had spread out of Mississippi across the South and into Arkansas. The Little Rock White Council arranged for Georgia Gov. Marvin Griffin to speak locally on August 22. Griffin vowed to resist integration in Georgia and asserted that if Governor Faubus stood up to the federal government, then Arkansas could remain segregated. So Griffin, who was staying overnight at the governor's mansion, put Faubus in a dilemma. The segregationists urged intervention to block desegregation while the moderates urged him instead to support the Blossom plan by issuing a statement, such as North Carolina Gov. Luther Hodges had made, that no violence would be tolerated.

Governor Faubus has always insisted that he never wanted to intervene in the local Little Rock school issue. Of course, he was reluctant to violate the first rule of politics—don't make waves, don't make enemies. Yet one should not accept the Faubus alibi as proof that he was not the villain of the Little Rock story. He did intervene and on the wrong side. No responsible leader should have stepped in unless persuaded that good results would have followed his decision. Certainly Faubus, who had never claimed to be a segregationist, did not act to preserve white supremacy. He had permitted desegregation in other schools without state interference.[11]

The governor's own explanation has been that he intervened only to prevent violence. But the secret information of planned violence, which he claimed to have, seemed a transparent sham then and has since been completely discredited. There were no runs on Little Rock knife and gun stores or convoys of violent segregationists coming to town, as he then asserted. This self-serving fabrication was immediately exposed by the *Arkansas Gazette* and confirmed, years later, by the opened records of the FBI. Faubus intervened in Little Rock for political reasons, to endear himself to those Arkansas whites who wanted desegregation stopped. The motivation of the governor never really had been a mystery. Faubus had been candid with former governor Sid McMath and AIDC director Winthrop Rockefeller: He needed an emotional issue to win the third term. He made the choice between furthering his political career and pushing the development of the state. "I'm sorry," he told Rockefeller, "but I'm already committed. I'm going to run for a third term, and if I don't do this, Jim Johnson and Bruce Bennett will tear me to shreds."[12] He selfishly put his own interests above those of the people of Arkansas, beginning the Faubusite insurrection against the Little Rock School Board and the federal government without hopes of winning anything except personal advantage.

The Faubusite insurrection began on September 3, 1957, with the Arkansas National Guard surrounding Central High to prevent the nine blacks from attending Central. It continued for seventeen days before Faubus submitted to a federal court injunction and removed the guard on September 20. A peaceful desegregation, which might have occurred had Faubus not intervened, was now impossible because media attention had further inflamed passions and insured that an angry crowd of white segregationists would prove more than the city police could handle. The white mob violence, when the nine blacks entered Central High on September 23, caused a reluctant President Eisenhower to send in the 101st Airborne Division to guarantee that mob action would not succeed in carrying out Governor Faubus' efforts to defy federal law.

Federal occupation of Central, along with the national media's criticism of white Little Rock, created a believing local audience for Faubus's efforts to revive Jeff Davis's rhetorical campaign against the outside Yankee conspiracy. In this campaign Faubus did, of course, retreat before federal power, but maintained a rear guard guerrilla war against sinister outside forces, keeping the race issue alive. He even stooped to charging that federal troops had invaded the dressing rooms of high school girls and he eliminated Brooks Hays from Congress because the moral man in politics had finally counseled against political expediency. In 1958 the Faubus forces defeated Hays just as Faubus surely could have eliminated even powerful Congressman Wilbur Mills, Senator J. William Fulbright, or Senator John McClellan, had they dared to criticize.

The governor's encouragement of segregationists helped to make school terrifying for the nine black students at Central who were harassed and intimidated by those the governor had encouraged to believe integration could be overturned. The assistant principal, Elizabeth Huckaby, made the Faubus responsibility clear when she wrote: "The governor will have to bear the major blame—for these children, for a crippled school for eighteen hundred others, for fear, hate, and suspicion in a community and state, and for a disrupted economy in Arkansas and comfort to the international rivals of the United States."[13]

Despite enormous national and substantial local criticism, the Faubus strategy worked politically. He assumed heroic proportions to white citizens across the state who applauded wildly in the belief that the governor was standing up for Arkansas and the rights of white parents. At public gatherings little old ladies rushed up to hug Faubus and promise "If you wanta run ten times we'll be for you every time." With the majority supporting his defiance of the federal courts, even the rebukes of the *Arkansas Gazette* could be turned to advantage. The *Gazette's* 85-year-old proprietor, J.N. Heiskell, who cared more for his conscience and his community than his profits, had given editor Harry Ashmore freedom to publish the most vigorous and continuing argument against the course followed by Governor Faubus. This journalistic crusade won two Pulitzer prizes but cost the *Gazette* eighteen percent of its circulation and more than a million dollars in net income as Faubus forces organized a boycott of reading and advertising in the *Gazette*. A new auto bumper sticker "*Gazette* Ad, Too Bad" warned firms against using the morning paper.[14]

Faubus campaigned for a third term as a simple mountaineer who would save the Arkansas people from the *Gazette* and from sinister outside forces determined to force unwarranted aggression. These sinister forces, such as the NAACP, were using *Gazette* editor Harry Ashmore and other "quislings" and "fifth column men" to defame the governor's Little Rock decision. But Faubus would never surrender. There had been only two possible decisions at Little Rock, he said, one course had been to "do what the federals did—go ahead and knock people in the head." The other, the Faubus action, had been to use the guard "to preserve the peace by keeping the schools segregated." Faubus now candidly admitted he had used the guard to defend segregation. And he would close his campaign by holding up a copy of editor Harry Ashmore's book, *An Epitaph for Dixie,* declaring the voters' choice to be between the *Gazette* editor who would "bury the South we know" and himself who would never surrender to outside interference but lead towards "even brighter pages in the history of the state."[15]

During the campaign three former governors of the state stepped forward to recommend against a Faubus election because he had created a national tragedy which gave propaganda for the Soviet Union to use in Africa and the Third World. Sid McMath even purchased a half-hour of television to suggest that Faubus had lacked courage enough to face the Little Rock mob and announce that the issue would be resolved by normal government processes. He had personally urged his old friend not to block desegregation, but "Faubus stated frankly and brazenly that he needed an emotional issue to overcome the tradition against a third term." So Faubus had grabbed for fame and power, McMath charged, by shouting defiance against the United States, setting race against race, and neighbor against neighbor. Even though the liberal Democrat McMath had been raised a segregationist, he said, he could not defy the United States of America. "I have always thrilled at the sight of the Stars and Stripes. . . . I cannot tread on that flag." But on election day the Arkansas voters, or 69 percent of them, did vote for the man who had violated a federal school desegregation order.[16]

Governor Faubus closed down the high schools of Little Rock for the 1958–59 school year to avoid integration and still the local voters did not object. Not until the spring of 1959 when the bankers began to worry that not a single new industrial plant had recently chosen to locate in Little Rock, did the business community begin to organize against Faubus and the segregationists. During the seven years before Little Rock became the international symbol of racial controversy, a steady industrial expansion had brought in forty outside companies. In just eight months before the riot, eight new plants with 1002 new jobs moved into the capital city. Following the Faubus insurrection, however, no industry wanted to come to Little Rock. As the months passed without promise of new industrial development, the business elite felt compelled to move the city away from the position of massive resistance towards integration.[17]

An opportunity for the business elite emerged in May 1959,

when the three segregationist board members proposed to purge from the teaching and administrative faculty all who believed in integration. The business, civic, and professional leaders moved on May 7 to organize STOP (Stop This Outrageous Purge). Rather than candidly supporting integration, the committee talked only of opposing the purge. The segregationists counterorganized with CROSS (Committee to Retain Our Segregated Schools) and enlisted the aid of Faubus in fighting the "Cadillac Brigade" and the "left wing country club" integrationist conspiracy. The moderate establishment won the May 25 recall elections, unseating the segregationist board members, and putting Little Rock back on the road to moderation.

After the white upper classes united with black voters to move Little Rock toward desegregation, the crafty Orval Faubus also gradually shifted away from the segregationists. In his 1960 reelection campaign, Little Rock integration and the *Arkansas Gazette* played only a minor role in his speeches. He so disappointed the White Citizens Council by refusing to block further integration, that they ran Dale Alford against him two years later. Faubus claimed to be the moderate in 1962, attacked from the right by Alford and from the left by McMath. He took the role of a successful political boss, avoiding controversial issues and asking only that his political machine and the voters "Keep Arkansas' Program of Proven Progress." The voters reelected Faubus for a total of six terms before he retired undefeated in 1966.[18]

Orval Faubus proved himself the most skillful politician in the history of the state. No other politician won six terms. His skills were devoted to retaining personal power rather than providing wise leadership. His defiance of federal power and the moral sense of the nation made the state again a symbol of contempt without gaining advantage for any but Orval Faubus. Had he sought to provide intelligent leadership by surrendering to the inevitable, perhaps he would only have gone down in defeat. Yet, at least, the historian could write that he had tried. Now we can only conclude that he took the detour back towards Dixie rather than lead into the modern Arkansas.

11

Cinderella Time

By the 1970s Arkansas experienced a reversal of fortunes as dramatic as the Cinderella fairy tale in which a miserable drudge turned into a beautiful princess because merit and beauty were finally recognized. So long the object of amusement and contempt Arkansas finally excited the envy of northeastern states as new population, industry, and investment moved in to make her a part of the new growth frontier of America, increasing her population by 18.8 percent during the 1970s. Arkansans proudly proclaimed their transformation: "Twenty-five years ago Arkansas was part of the 'Old South' clinging to an agrarian way of life and a racist social order. Today, Arkansas is part of the Sun Belt which offers the promise of good climate, plenty of water, and the availability of energy."[1]

The emergence of the new Arkansas seemed to follow Winthrop Rockefeller's arrival from New York in 1953. He constructed his Winrock Farm showplace, built Little Rock's first glass skyscraper, attracted 90,000 new industrial jobs, and became the first Republican governor since Reconstruction. By unstinting use of his energy and personal fortune Rockefeller did more to revitalize Arkansas than any other individual. Yet the economic and historical forces which were bringing increased prosperity to Arkansas were never created by a single man.

The state ceased to be so poor when most Arkansans left farming. Agriculture ceased to be a drag on state statistics because three-fourths of those employed on the land in 1950 left farming during the next twenty years. A mere seven percent of the work force remained in agriculture. Those who remained on the shrinking number of farms made themselves far more productive. With machinery and chemicals the lowland planters annually produced a billion dollar crop of soybeans, rice, and cotton. Planters entered agribusiness; they processed and marketed their own grain through their cooperative Riceland Foods, which sold more than half a billion dollars of grain a year and dominated markets in Western Europe and elsewhere. The upland farmers remained in agriculture only by getting out of row crops and turning to chickens and cattle. Broilers became the number two crop in Arkansas which combined with eggs amounted to almost a billion dollars in sales annually. Farm income grew dramatically and farmers felt like bulls on Wall Street as they watched rural land prices spiral upward from the reasonable $25 to $75 an acre prices of the 1950s. By the seventies even upland farmers were afraid to put a price of $1000 per acre on land for fear "some fool just might buy it." This stimulating appreciation in farm prices enhanced the rural love of the land and of farming, making most farmers determined to keep the land in the family as a precious part of the Arkansas heritage.[2]

The ruthless market forces which had driven most Arkansans from farming also brought in new manufacturing with higher pay scales. Manufacturing accompanied the American population which shifted towards the Sunbelt, drawn to the southeast and the southwest by federal defense and space spending as well as the warmer climate. Even though the central six states of the South were slower to participate in the Sunbelt boom, they offered plant locations near the new growth centers. With cheaper land, labor, and transportation costs, a new Arkansas plant made more economic sense than one in the northeast or even one in the booming centers. So Whirlpool shifted its refrigerator plant from Michigan to Fort Smith, and Carrier Corporation built a new central air conditioning plant at Maumelle not only because of the friendly business climate and the work force potential but especially because it was "close to our rapidly growing air conditioning business in the South, Southwest, and West."[3] Arkansas manufacturing employment spurted ahead, becoming the eighth fastest in rate of growth. The workers employed in manufacturing grew to 24 percent of the state work force, one point higher than the national average.

No longer did lumber head the list as the major industrial employer. Georgia-Pacific, Weyerhauser, and Potlatch continued to be major employers; but by 1980 the lumber industry, employing 22,441, fell to third place while employment in processing food—meat, poultry, eggs, dairy, fruit, grain, and vegetables—employing 30,923 Arkansans, rose to first place. Second place went to the new electric and electronic industry which employed 23,957 workers building motors, refrigerators, and televisions. Arkansas no longer served as a simple supplier of raw materials; now her industrial mix included every stage of the manufacturing process and a wide variety of industrial products. In the aluminum industry, Reynolds Metals operated the entire cycle of mining, refining, manufacturing, and recycling within the state. The *Directory of Arkansas Manufacturers* included not only the low-wage clothing industry but also the higher paying paper, chemical, and petroleum industries where workers were paid six and seven dollars an hour.[4]

Arkansas had climbed from 50 to 79 percent of the American per capita income during the generation since the Second World War, gaining so rapidly that even a Little Rock bank officer talked of the "inevitability" of a wealthy Arkansas. Even if the citizens perversely tried to stop economic growth by retaining the archaic state constitution with its ten percent interest ceiling, Edward Penick of First Arkansas Bankstock Corporation said, the developing shift of wealth from the North to Arkansas and the South would continue. The state's attractive natural resources—oil, gas, bauxite, timber, land, and water—along with her probusiness labor force, would continue to attract wealth-producing industry, entrepreneurs, managers, and technicians.[5]

Retirees also flooded into Arkansas from the midwest. The Ozarks became a new regional center for elderly migrants who wanted to leave the snowbanks and traffic of Chicago to live in retirement communities on an Arkansas lake. Some bought elegant homes but others moved into one of the squadrons of mobile homes along dirt roads. Here they maintained something of their old neighborhood communities, living among people from their old city back in Illinois, Iowa, or Nebraska. The state became second only to Florida in its percentage of the elderly, reaching 13.7 percent while Baxter County hit 28 percent by 1980. Even a few migrants from St. Petersburg began turning up in Bull Shoals because increasing noise, congestion, and costs—the quality of life—drove them to abandon Florida for Arkansas.[6] The elderly brought money and social security checks, contributing to the general state prosperity, although they also tended to oppose state and local taxation.

In urban America, where the quality of life now deteriorated, rural and small town living ceased to be regarded as disreputable, becoming instead something to be cherished and supported. The antiurban trend had its outer rim extremists, the urban dropouts of the sixties who went "back to the land"and established rural communes to escape urban hassle and confusion. They were followed by the survivalists who sought to escape racial riots, economic chaos, and nuclear war by buying guns and rations to store in rural retreats. But the mainstream nature of the reverse movement became clear in the 1980 census which revealed that across America the rural and small towns, for the first time since 1820, were growing more rapidly than the urban areas.

The new respect for rural America had been fully exploited by sharp-eyed entrepreneurs of Mountain View who took advantage of the new solicitiousness and hustled a $3.4 million federal grant for a national folk culture center in their primitive county seat where Jimmy Driftwood is said once to have gathered the banjo, dulcimer, and guitar players around the old pot-bellied stove of the Stone County courthouse.[7] The real purpose of the Mountain View folk center was to lure the tourists in to support mountain music and provide comfortable livings for the native craftsmen who displayed woodcarving and other pioneer wares for sale in the cedar buildings of the Ozark Foothills Handicraft Guild.

The national interest in preserving the past was also tapped to save the Buffalo River from dams and development. For more than a hundred miles the Buffalo ran freely through the rugged terrain of the Ozark mountain counties of Newton, Searcy, and Marion before joining the White River in Baxter County. The preservationists and conservationists joined against the land owners and the dam developers, persuading Congress to make the Buffalo a national river in 1972, buying up the land for the National Park Service to maintain the free flowing stream in its natural state for the enjoyment of future generations. So the Buffalo joined the state's already extensive national forests–the Ozark and the Ouachita National Forests.[8]

While much of the natural landscape became preserved in its primitive condition, the population emerged as modern Americans who altered the face of their state politics, eliminating relics of the age of Dixie. The Supreme Court reapportionment decisions were of immense help in changing the state legislature as Richard Yates has illustrated, using Perry County's representative as an example.

> Paul Van Dalsem of Perry County was a dominant and domineering figure in the House. Possessed of a bullhorn voice, an irascible temper, and a disposition to start unseemly legislative brawls, he contributed generously to the disrepute into which the legislature fell. In the summer of 1963, he addressed a Little Rock civic club, and in the course of his remarks his mind fell upon a subject which promised amusement to a male audience— women in politics, especially some Little Rock women who had lobbied during the recent session of the legislature. "They're frustrated," he said. "We don't have any of these university women in Perry County, but I'll tell you what we do up there when one of our women starts poking around in something she doesn't know anything about: we get her an extra milk cow. If that don't work, we give her a little more garden to tend to. And then if that's not enough, we get her pregnant and keep her barefoot."[9]

Press reports of the representative's rural-chauvinist humor angered Little Rock women; when reapportionment united Perry and Pulaski counties into the same legislative district in 1965, urban women organized and eliminated Van Dalsem from the legislature.

The old politics of Dixie also disappeared from the governors' office in the sixties. Orval Faubus had been cartooned into a laughingstock by Little Rock artist George Fisher who made him a symbol of power politics and political expediency. When Faubus dropped

out in 1966 the voters elected Winthrop Rockefeller who spoke the
national language. Four years later the voters demonstrated the
permanence of their return to mainstream America by replacing
Rockefeller not with an old style Dixie Democrat but with Dale
Bumpers, a small-town attorney with a Northwestern University
law degree who personified the new Sunbelt leadership. A new
generation of political leaders—Bumpers, David Pryor, Bill Clin-
ton, Jim Guy Tucker, Ray Thornton, and Frank White—surely represented the new face of Arkansas.[10]

As the old politics of race retreated into the past, Little Rock
emerged as a model of American racial success. The former symbol
of racial bigotry became a media example of an urban community
where the integrated schools worked with racial harmony and outstanding Scholastic Aptitude Test scores. When CBS finally filmed
a television drama of the 1957 diary of assistant principal Elizabeth
Huckaby, the story was cast as the ancient racist history of a Little
Rock which had long changed. Blacks agreed that they had pro-
gressed in jobs and human dignity. Little Rock had been the only
southern city to appoint a black to manage its airport and in 1981
the white majority elected a black mayor, Charles Bussey. Yes, blacks
said "there had been a growth of human dignity among black
Americans in Arkansas." And yes, "Arkansas is the 'land of opportunity,' its been that for me."[11]

Change and transformation in the Cinderella state, however
never entirely erased those cultural patterns associated with an earlier day. The population remained largely one of rural and small-
town people, despite the federal Census Bureau's conclusion that
a majority of the 2,285,513 Arkansans were urban in 1980. Little
Rock counted 158,461 residents but Fort Smith, North Little Rock,
and Pine Bluff all remained below 70,000 in population. The urbanites in Arkansas distributed themselves largely in small cities
and towns where traditional absolute values persisted. In the face
of any change, rural and small-town minds retained the traditional
folk values. Conservative evangelical protestantism continued its
dominance despite the move of mainline churches to theological
liberalism. As United Methodism grew more liberal, for example,
individual Arkansans dropped out to join fundamentalist congregations. In an unusually dramatic departure, one-fifth of the 1500

members of the First United Methodist Church in Jonesboro withdrew in 1980 from liberal religion to retreat to a more conservative faith.[12]

Arkansas Baptists kept more in touch with popular religion by stressing the old evangelism while avoiding theological modernism. Baptists recruited almost one fourth of the state's population as members of their faith. "The all-prevailing Baptist church, as well as its direct descendant, the Pentecostal," John Gould Fletcher's *Arkansas* complained, kept "minds narrow" and had been "fatal to all intellectual advancement." But even Baptists changed after World War II, accepting more of the outside world, putting in stained glass windows while discarding the old censorious custom of dismissing members found guilty of dancing, drinking, smoking, playing cards, going to the movies, cursing, gambling, or living indiscreetly. Congregational exclusions were no longer reported after 1945 as the Baptist churches narrowed their social attack to drinking and gambling, while accepting the congregational comforts of organs, padded pews, carpeted floors, printed bulletins, choir robes and directors, nurseries, and educated pastors. While permitting more worldly behavior, Arkansas Baptists rigidly resisted any alteration of the belief that they were the one true Christian faith. When Jeff Davis's old congregation, First Baptist of Russellville, reconsidered the New Testament sacraments and agreed to permit communion with non-Baptists and even accept the legitimacy of their baptism, the hostile Arkansas State Baptist Convention ousted them from the denomination in November of 1965. For at least a decade those congregations who endorsed the heresies of open communion, alien immersion, or the World Council of Churches were refused admission to the State Convention. Yet more than forty percent of the faithful consistently voted to accept the ecumenical Russellville Baptists. So Baptists, too, struggled among themselves over tradition and innovation. First Baptist in Arkadelphia even ordained the state's first two women as Baptist deacons and the Arkansas Baptists collected their first hunger offering in 1977.[13]

For those who accused the major denominations of compromising with the devil and permitting a breakdown of traditional values, the antievolution crusade of 1981 offered hope of restoring morality. The Arkansas Moral Majority of conservative evangelicals lobbied their Creation-Science Bill 590 through the state legislature in March of 1981, requiring school teachers to give equal time to the Biblical account that God created the universe no more than 10,000 years ago. A majority of Arkansans likely agreed that the spiritually wicked theory of evolution should not be permitted to undermine biblical literalism and the authority of evangelical Christianity, but the newspaper editors of large and small towns complained "the thoughtless bozos of the legislature had again made Arkansas a national joke." The urban editors were joined by mainline Methodist, Presbyterian, Southern Baptist, Episcopal, and Roman Catholic leaders who, with the American Civil Liberties Union, appealed the issue to the Federal Court for a first rate seminar on science and theology. Then Judge William R. Overton, from Little Rock, struck down the law as a legislative attempt to establish religion in violation of the constitutional separation of church and state. The Little Rock establishment and the federal courts thus overturned a popular folk effort which had been approved by almost eighty percent of the legislature.[14]

While boosters and intellectuals may have embraced the latest fashions in ideas and causes, rural and small-town Arkansans usually remained anchored in a traditional world of familiar values. Distrustful of modernism, old-style Arkansans preferred the familiar in ideas and people to the new. This reassertion of religious conservatism offered evidence in support of somber warnings from University of Arkansas Distinguished History Professor Willard B. Gatewood, Jr., that neither Cinderella metaphors nor Sunbelt myths should be trusted to free Arkansas of the burden of the past. Traditional religion, culture, and economics are persistant. With a wise historian's skepticism of the euphoria of the seventies, Gatewood cautioned against the mindless belief that all the region's ills would be automatically cured by the sun. To avoid yet another cycle of booster belief followed by bitter disillusionment, Gatewood stressed that mythmakers and image merchants should never be permitted to obscure the truth that Arkansas had not yet overcome statistical disparities with sister states. Nor should an unselective hunger for Sunbelt wealth cause Arkansans to permit undesirable crowding, pollution, urban blight, and despoiled landscapes which could surely ruin the "good life" of small-town, genial Arkansas. While Sunbelt Arkansas might seem on the "threshold of fulfillment," Gatewood warned that equally promising illusions had repeatedly misled citizens of the state.[15]

The glow on the Sunbelt did fade a little as the depression of the 1980s hit lumber, agriculture, and manufacturing, driving local unemployment to 12.3 percent, higher than the national average. High interest rates and low commodity prices forced farmers into the worst financial crisis since the Great Depression. Even a few major manufacturing plants, such as the Singer Sewing Machine cabinet factory employing 600 workers in Trumann, closed permanently. Hurricane Creek, the aluminum plant in the little town of Bauxite, which had led the new industrialization during World War II, closed, eliminating 700 of the state's better paying jobs. Yet even with more than 114,000 Arkansas workers unemployed, the state's industrial development director maintained that the state had continued to attract new industry and had more than held its own with competing Sunbelt states.[16]

Arkansas has not yet risen above 49th place in either per capita income or support for public education.[17] Thoughtful Arkansans worry that, without more commitment to schooling a new generation of workers, the state cannot participate in the new computer technology revolution, but will lag behind with a labor intensive and largely extractive industrialization. The state's quality-of-life rankings rate no better than 44th place in America and many areas have not yet escaped a traditional look of poverty. And yet the Sunbelt cheerleaders were not entirely false. Americans now like Arkansas: they have moved in to enjoy its rural landscape, they have chosen a Miss Arkansas to become Miss America. A homegrown department store chain, Wal-Mart Stores, has been rated by Wall Street as one of the five best managed companies in America. Even in a depression, Arkansans are enjoying a greater recognition and prosperity than in the past. Jobs in the low-wage chicken processing industry have even become so unattractive to Arkansans that Pilgrim Industries of DeQueen has had to hire new immigrants from Mexico to complete its work force. Mexican-Americans as well as Asian-Americans are now creating a more pluralistic Arkansas society. While Arkansas can boast of nuclear power generators and

Titan missile silos, the state has also produced peace movement leaders urging a nuclear freeze and an eventual worldwide disarmament. Both Arkansas senators have supported the peace movement while the state's most famous immigrant from New England, pediatrician Dr. Benjamin Spock, explains that boys reared in a less macho fashion would better understand the wisdom of women who support the nuclear freeze. Arkansas males, at least those in Little Rock, can accept female leadership. The capital city has moved from electing a black male city mayor to electing a white female, Susan Fleming. Change and diversity are everywhere in Arkansas along with the traditional past. So here, as elsewhere, the struggle between the old and the new, tradition and change, persists.

Notes
Bibliography

Notes

1 The New Country

1. James G. Leyburn *The Scotch-Irish: A Social History;* Richard A. Bartlett, *The New Country: A Social History of the American Frontier 1776-1890,* pp. 134–140.

2. Russell W. Benedict, "Story of an Early Settlement in Central Arkansas,"ed. Ted R. Worley, *Arkansas Historical Quarterly* 10 (Summer 1951): 117–137; Frank L. Owsley "The Pattern of Migration and Settlement on the Southern Frontier," *Journal of Southern History* 11 (May 1945): 147–176.

3. Walter N. Vernon, *Methodism in Arkansas 1816-1976,* p. 13.

4. Forrest McDonald and Grady McWhiney, "The Antebellum Southern Herdsman: A Reinterpretation," *Journal of Southern History* 41 (May 1975): 147–166; Henry R. Schoolcraft, *A View of the Lead Mines of Missouri,* pp. 256–257; Friedrich Gerstaecker, *Wild Sports in the Far West,* ed. Edna L. and Harrison Steeves, pp. 164–165, 168.

5. Richard G. Lillard, *The Great Forest;* Bartlett, *The New Country,* p. 176–180; Gerstaecker, *Wild Sports in the Far West,* p. 165; Glenn G. Martel, "Early Days in Columbia County,"*Arkansas Historical Quarterly* 2 (September 1943): 214–219; Nathan D. Smith letter to Baltimore *Farmer and Gardener,* February 10, 1835, p. 322.

6. Robert B. Walz, "Migration into Arkansas," *Arkansas Historical Quarterly* 17 (Winter 1958): 309–324.

7. John Ferguson, "William E. Woodruff and the Territory of Arkansas 1819–1836"; Margaret Rose, *Arkansas Gazette: The Early Years 1819-1866,* pp. 3–42.

8. *Arkansas State Gazette,* December 9, 1840.

9. *Little Rock Gazette & Democrat,* August 13, 1852; Malcolm J. Rohrbough, *The Trans-Appalachian Frontier,* p. 277.

10. Orville W. Taylor, *Negro Slavery in Arkansas*, pp. 47–58.

11. George P. Rawick, *The American Slave: A Composite Autobiography* vol. 11, pp. 144–145.

12. Josiah H. Shinn, *Pioneers and Makers of Arkansas*, pp. 256–257.

13. Rohrbough, *The Trans-Appalachian Frontier*, p. 397; Dwight Pitcaithley, "Settlement of the Arkansas Ozarks: The Buffalo River Valley," *Arkansas Historical Quarterly* 37 (Autumn 1978): 203–222.

2 Redeeming the People

1. William F. Pope, *Early Days in Arkansas*, pp. 223–225; *Gazette*, May 23, 30, June 20, 1838.

2. Charles Giles Bridle Dauberry, *Journal of a Tour Through the United States 1837-38*, pp. 150–168; Theodore Dwight Weld, *American Slavery as it is: Testimony of a Thousand Witnesses* (New York: American Anti-Slavery Society, 1839), pp. 188–190; Lonnie White, *Politics on the Southwestern Frontier: Arkansas Territory 1819–1836*, pp. 67–87, 203–204; Waddy William Moore, "Territorial Arkansas, 1819–1836," pp. 252–282.

3. Mrs. Thomas Campbell, "Two Letters of the Meek Family, Union County 1842–1845," *Arkansas Historical Quarterly* 15 (Autumn 1956): 260–266; *Gazette and Democrat*, October 27, 1854.

4. Hiram Abiff Whittington to his brother, April 21, 1827, December 1, 1828, May 13, 1830, reprinted in *Arkansas Gazette*, April 17, 1932; Margaret Smith Ross, ed. "Letters of Hiram Abiff Whittington 1827–1834,"*Pulaski County Historical Society*, no. 3 (December 1956), pp. 1–59.

5. U.S. Census Office, *Statistics of the United States in 1860*, (Washington: G.P.O., 1866), pp. 355–356; Josiah H. Shinn, *Pioneers and Makers of Arkansas*, pp. 48–49.

6. Walter N. Vernon, *William Stevenson: Riding Preacher*, pp. 1–35; Vernon, *Methodism in Arkansas 1816–1976*, pp. 17-21.

7. J.S. Rogers, *History of Arkansas Baptists*, pp. 117–120, 181–185; W. E. McLeod, "Early Baptist Movements in Northeast Arkansas," *Arkansas Historical Quarterly* 5 (Summer 1946): 154–168.

8. Walter Brownlow Posey, *The Baptist Church in the Lower Mississippi Valley 1776-1845* (Lexington: University of Kentucky Press, 1957), p. 15–19, 38–53; E. Glenn Hinson, *A History of Baptists in Arkansas, 1818–1978*, pp. 14–16, 24–26.

9. Missionary Baptist Records, Box 2, Special Collections, University of Arkansas Library, Fayetteville; Donald G. Mathews, *Religion in the Old South*, pp. 40–43.

10. Pope, *Early Days in Arkansas*, pp. 210, 292.

11. Orville W. Taylor, *Negro Slavery in Arkansas*, pp. 176–177, 180–181; Taylor, "Baptists and Slavery in Arkansas: Relationships and Attitudes," *Arkansas Historical Quarterly* 38 (Autumn 1979): 215; After Silas Toncray moved from Little Rock to Memphis he built his own chapel in 1837 where he preached to a predominantly black congregation, David M. Tucker, *Black Pastors·and Leaders: Memphis, 1819–1972*, (Memphis: Memphis State University Press, 1975), pp. 4–5.

12. Vernon, *Methodism in Arkansas*, pp. 38–40.

13. Mathews, *Religion in the Old South*, pp. 191–219; Laurence W. Levine, *Black Culture and Black Consciousness* (New York: Oxford University Press, 1977), pp. 30–55.

14. Ferguson, "William E. Woodruff and the Territory of Arkansas," pp. 37–38, 55, 134–135.

15. Elmo Howell, "Mark Twain's Arkansas,"*Arkansas Historical Quarterly* 29 (Autumn 1970): 195–208; Norris W. Yates, *William T. Porter and the Spirit of the Times: A Study of the Big Bear School of Humor* (Baton Rouge: Louisiana State University Press, 1957). p. 121.

3 The Planter Sting

1. W. B. Worthen, *Early Banking in Arkansas*, pp.4–5; James Roger Sharp, *The Jacksonians Versus the Banks: Politics in the States after the Panic of 1837*, p. 36; William M. Gouge & William R. Miller, *Report of the Accountants . . . to Invesitgate the Affairs of the Real Estate Bank of Arkansas*, p. 53.

2. Worthen, *Early Banking in Arkansas*, p. 4.

3. Sevier to Jackson, April 4, 1836, in Clarence Edwin Carter, *The Territorial Papers of the United States*, vol. 21, *Arkansas, 1829–1836*, p. 1207.

4. Ted R. Worley, "The Control of the Real Estate Bank of the State of Arkansas 1836–55,"*Mississippi Valley Historical Review* 37 (December 1950): 412.

5. Ibid., 404.

6. Ibid., 409.

7. Reginald C. McGrane, *Foreign Bondholders and American State Debts*, pp. 245–257.

8. Ibid., 257-258.

9.Melinda Meek, "The Life of Archibald Yell,"*Arkansas Historical Quarterly* 26 (Fall 1967): 226–243; Worley, "The Control of the Real Estate Bank"pp. 419–426.

10. McGrane, *Foreign Bondholders and American State Debts*, p. 258.

11. U.S. Census 1860 (Manuscript on microfilm); *Biographical and Historical Memoirs of Southern Arkansas* (Chicago: Goodspeed, 1892), p. 1074; Gouge and Miller, *Report of the Accountants*, pp. 29, 37, 118.

12. T. M. Stinnett and Clara B. Kennan, *All This and Tomorrow Too*, pp. 17–21.

4 The Civil War

1. John M. Harrell, *Arkansas*, vol. 10 in Clement A. Evans, ed. *Confederate Military History*, p. 4.

2. Michael B. Dougan, *Confederate Arkansas: The People and Policies of a Frontier State in Wartime*, p. 61; Walter L. Brown, "Rowing Against the Stream: The Course of Albert Pike from National Whig to Secessionist,"*Arkansas Historical Quarterly 39* (Autumn 1980): 241–242; Robert L. Duncan, *Reluctant General: The Life and Times of Albert Pike* (New York: E.P. Dutton & Co., 1961), pp. 166–167.

3. George H. Thompson, *Arkansas and Reconstruction: The Influence of Geography, Economics, and Personality*, p. 29; David Y. Thomas, *Arkansas in War and Reconstruction*, pp. 65–66.

4. John L. Ferguson, ed. *Arkansas and the Civil War* (Little Rock: Pioneer Press, 1965), pp. 322–323, 521–522.

5. Chris Catalfamo-Serio, "The Effect of the Civil War on Ozark Culture" (mimeographed) (Prairie Grove: Cavanaugh, 1979), pp. 128–129.

6. Albert Castel, *General Sterling Price and the Civil War in the West*, pp. 66–76.

7. Robert G. Hartje, *Van Dorn* (Nashville: Vanderbilt University Press, 1967), pp. 117–161; Dougan, *Confederate Arkansas*, p. 87.

8. Bobby L. Roberts, "General T. C. Hindman and the Trans-Mississippi District," *Arkansas Historical Quarterly* 32 (Winter 1973): 303–304.

9. Stephen B. Oates, "The Prairie Grove Campaign, 1862," *Arkansas Historical Quarterly* 19 (Summer 1960): 119–141.

10. James Gill interview in George P. Rawick, *The American Slave: A Composite Autobiography* vol. 9, pt. 3, p. 24; Maude Carmichael, "Federal Experiments with Negro Labor on Abandoned Plantations in Arkansas: 1862–1865," *Arkansas Historical Quarterly* 1 (March 1942): 101–116.

11. Dougan, *Confederate Arkansas*, p. 119; John Quincy Wolf, Jr., ed. *Life in the Leatherwoods*, p. 9.

12. Murphy to A. Lincoln, February 17, 1863, reel 49, A. Lincoln Papers, Presidential Papers on Microfilm; John I. Smith, *The Courage of a Southern Unionist: A Biography of Isaac Murphy*.

13. Murphy to C. C. Bliss, September 26, 1863, reel 59, Lincoln Papers.

14. Murphy to Lincoln, January 23, 1864, reel 66; March 27, 1864, reel 71; April 11, April 22, 1864, reel 72; July 23, 1864, reel 78, December 13, 1864, reel 89, Lincoln Papers.

15. *Arkansas Gazette*, May 20, 1865.

16. Susan Briceland Fletcher, "Civil War Experience," Special Collections, University of Arkansas Library, Fayetteville; Minos Miller to mother, September 1, 1865, Minos Miller Manuscripts, Folder 6, Special Collections, University of Arkansas Library.

5 Carpetbaggers

1. *Arkansas Gazette*, November 17, 1978.

2. Thomas S. Staples, *Reconstruction in Arkansas 1862-1874*, pp. 109–114.

3. Powell Clayton, *The Aftermath of the Civil War in Arkansas*, pp. 1–36.

4. Richard L. Hume, "The Arkansas Constitutional Convention of 1868: A Case Study in the Politics of Reconstruction," *Journal of Southern History* 39 (May 1973): 183–202.

5. Clayton, *The Aftermath of the Civil War in Arkansas*, pp. 38–49.

6. George H. Thompson, *Arkansas and Reconstruction*, pp. 231–233.

7. Clayton, *The Aftermath of the Civil War in Arkansas*, pp. 45–48; T.M. Stinnett & Clara B. Kennan, *All This and Tomorrow Too*, pp. 26–40; Robert A. Leflar, *The First 100 Years: Centennial History of the University of Arkansas*, pp. 1–20.

8. Clayton, *The Aftermath of the Civil War in Arkansas*, pp. 56–105; Allen W. Trelease, *White Terror: The Ku Klux Klan Conspiracy and Southern Reconstruction*, pp. 149–174; Howard C. Westwood, "The Federals' Cold Shoulder to Arkansas' Powell Clayton," *Civil War History* 26 (September 1980): 240–255.

9. *Arkansas Gazette*, August 14, 24, 1869; Staples, *Reconstruction in Arkansas*, pp. 375–376.

10. Martha Ann Ellenburg, "Reconstruction in Arkansas," p. 43.

11. "Arkansas' Iliad," *New York Herald*, September 30, October 5, 7, 8, 1872; Thomas J. Reynolds, "The Pope County Militia War," *Publications of the Arkansas Historical Association*, vol. 2, (Fayetteville, 1908): pp. 174–198. J. T. Bullock, "The Pope County Militia War," *Arkansas Valley Historical Papers* No. 33 (June 1965); John M. Harrell, *The Brooks and Baxter War: A History of the Reconstruction Period in Arkansas*, pp. 140–150.

12. *Arkansas Gazette*, February 3, 1875, July 2, 1878; W.M. Fishback, "Recon-

struction in Arkansas," in Hilary A. Herbert, ed., *Why the Solid South* (Baltimore: R. H. Woodward, 1890), pp. 284–320; David Y. Thomas, *Arkansas and its People*, pp. 152–153.

13. *Arkansas Gazette,* July 7, 1883.

6 Black Man's Place

1. Joseph M. St. Hilaire, "The Negro Delegates in the Arkansas Constitutional Convention of 1863: A Group Profile,"*Arkansas Historical Quarterly* 33 (Spring 1974): 38–69; *Arkansas Gazette* January 14, 1868.

2. Mifflin W. Gibbs, *Shadow and Light: An Autobiography,* pp. 1–136.

3. *Arkansas Gazette,* December 21, 1871, January 30, 1872.

4. Ibid., October 23, 1874.

5. Leon F. Litwack, *Been in the Storm So Long: The Aftermath of Slavery* (New York: Alfred A. Knopf, 1979) pp. 309–411; George P. Rawick, ed. *The American Slave: A Composite Autobiography* vol. 9, pt. 3, pp. 98–99; *Arkansas Gazette,* January 15, 1882, March 26, 1884; William Pickens, *Bursting Bonds,* pp. 7–31; Nell Irvin Painter, *Exodusters: Black Migration to Kansas after Reconstruction* (New York: Alfred A. Knopf, 1977), p.137.

6. Joe Tolbert Segraves, "Arkansas Politics, 1874-1918" pp. 111–114; M.W. Martin to M. E. Streiby, September 27, 1878, Arkansas reel 1, no. 4190, American Missionary Association Papers on Microfilm; Powell Clayton Speech to Lincoln Club, *Arkansas Gazette,* September 23, 1888.

7. *Arkansas Gazette,* July 12, 13, 17, 18, 1888.

8. Ibid., July 22, 1888.

9. John William Graves, "Negro Disfranchisement in Arkansas,"*Arkansas Historical Quarterly* 26 (Autumn 1967): 199–225; J. Morgan Kousser, *The Shaping of Southern Politics: Suffrage Restriction and the Establishment of the One-Party South, 1880-1910,* pp. 123–130, 261–265.

10. *Arkansas Gazette,* November 25, 1898.

11. Ibid., December 28, 1900, November 20, 1902, September 5 6, 1922; E.C. Morris, *Sermons, Addresses & Reminiscences* (Nashville: National Baptist Publishing Board, 1901); G.P. Hamilton, *Beacon Lights of the Race* (Memphis: E. H. Clarke & Brother, 1911), pp. 239–249.

12. William F. Holmes, "The Arkansas Cotton Pickers Strike of 1891 and the Demise of the Colored Farmer's Alliance," *Arkansas Historical Quarterly* 32 (Summer 1973): 107–119; William Warren Rogers, "Negro Knights of Labor in Arkansas,"*Labor History* 10 (Summer 1969): 498–505.

13. *Arkansas Gazette,* May 14, 15, 1892.

14. Ibid., January 14, 16, 1883, April 21, 1888, January 17, 1894, July 25, 1897, August 8, 1899.

15. Ibid., November 18, 1898, October 1, 1906.

16. Forney Hutchinson, *My Treasure Chest: An Indirect Autobiography* (Atlanta: Banner Press, 1943), pp. 31–32.

17. *Arkansas Gazette,* August 14, 18, 1898.

18. Ibid., January 11, 1906, January 29, 1907, January 12, 1908.

19. Ibid., August 31, 1904

20.Dan A. Rudd and Theo. Bond, *From Slavery to Wealth: The Life of Scott Bond* (Madison, Ark: Journal Printing Company, 1917); *Arkansas Gazette* August 13, 19, 1910.

21. *Arkansas Gazette,* June 18, 1905, October 16, 1913; Louis R. Harlan, ed., *The Booker T. Washington Papers* vol. 8 (Urbana: University of Illinois Press, 1979), pp. 440–443.

22. *Arkansas Gazette,* November 25, 1910.

7 The Politics of Poverty

1. C. Vann Woodward, *Origins of the New South,* pp. 175–187; John McDaniel Wheeler, "The People's Party in Arkansas, 1891–1896," pp. 1–80; Joe Tolbert Segraves, "Arkansas Politics, 1874–1918," pp. 163–197; W. Scott Morgan, *History of the Wheel and Alliance and the Impending Revolution,* pp. 13–60.

2. See Arkansas State Exposition Speeches in *Arkansas Gazette,* October 26, 1887; and state house articles, January 8, 1890, March 5, 1895, April 15, 1899.

3. Berton E. Henningson, Jr. "Northwest Arkansas and the Brothers of Freedom: The Roots of a Farmer Movement," *Arkansas Historical Quarterly* 34 (Winter 1975): 304–423; Morgan, *History of the Wheel and Alliance,* pp. 60–65; Clifton Paisley, "The Political Wheelers and Arkansas' Election of 1888," *Arkansas Historical Quarterly* 25 (Spring 1966): 3–21.

4. Segraves, "Arkansas Politics, 1874–1918," pp. 104–105; Richard L. Niswonger, "Arkansas Democratic Politics, 1896–1920," p. 90; Niswonger, "Daniel Webster Jones" in *The Governors of Arkansas: Essays in Political Biography,* ed. Timothy P. Donovan and Willard B. Gatewood, Jr., pp. 103–110; J. Morgan Kousser, *The Shaping of Southern Politics: Suffrage Restriction and the Establishment of the One-Party South, 1880–1910,* pp. 123–130.

5. Charles Jacobson, *The Life Story of Jeff Davis: The Stormy Petrel of Arkansas Politics,* pp. 45–60; Richard L. Niswonger, "A Study in Southern Demagoguery: Jeff Davis of Arkansas," *Arkansas Historical Quarterly* 39 (Summer 1980): 114–124.

6. George W. Donaghey, *Building a State Capitol,* pp. 39–44.

7. *Arkansas Gazette,* April 1, 1906; Jacobson, *The Life Story of Jeff Davis,* p. 63; Leland Duvall, *Arkansas: Colony and State,* pp. 177–178; Harry Lee Williams, *Behind the Scenes in Arkansas Politics,* (n.p., n.d.), p. 134.

8. Niswonger, "Arkansas Democratic Politics, 1896–1920," pp. 207–209; *Arkansas Gazette,* April 24, May 29, 1902, April 1, 1906.

9. John Lee Eighmy, *Churches in Cultural Captivity: A History of Social Attitudes of Southern Baptists* (Knoxville: University of Tennessee Press, 1972), pp. 55, 69, 70–71; Rufus B. Spain, *At Ease in Zion: Social History of Southern Baptists* (Nashville: Vanderbilt University Press, 1967), pp. 210–213; U.S. Bureau of Census, *A Compendium of the Ninth Census: 1870* (Washington: Government Printing Office, 1872), pp. 518–519; U.S. Bureau of Census *Religious Bodies, 1936,* vol. 1 (Washington: Government Printing Office, 1941), pp. 377, 405–408; E. Glenn Hinson, *A History of Baptists in Arkansas,* p. 113, interprets Davis as representing the "poorly educated, reactionary, backwoods element," while James P. Eagle spoke for the more progressive Arkansas Baptists.

10. *Arkansas Gazette,* April 1, 1906.

11. L. S. Dunaway, *Jeff Davis: Governor and United States Senator,* p. 42; *Arkansas Gazette,* May 25, 1904.

12. *Arkansas Gazette,* August 7, 1904.

13. Segraves, "Arkansas Politics, 1874–1918," pp. 300–304.

14. L. A. Markham, "Present-Day Impressions of Rural Arkansas Life," *Arkansas Gazette,* June 20, September 19, December 12, 1915; Daniel Boone Lackey,

"Cutting and Floating Red Cedar Logs in North Arkansas," *Arkansas Historical Quarterly* 19 (Winter 1960): 361–370; Not all mountaineers were grateful for the work; Orval Faubus's father became a socialist because of resentment over being paid only ten cents a tie, (*Arkansas Gazette,* February 16, 1964).

15. *Arkansas Gazette,* June 7, 1904, November 7, 1908, September 1, 1912; Boyce House, "A Small Arkansas Town 50 years Ago," *Arkansas Historical Quarterly* 18 (Autumn 1959): 291–307.

16. Segraves, "Arkansas Politics, 1874–1918", pp. 352–355.

17. Niswonger, "Arkansas Democratic Politics, 1896–1920," pp. 335–345.

18. Harry S. Ashmore, *An Epitaph for Dixie* (New York: W. W. Norton, 1957), p. 151; Raymond O. Arsenault, "Jeff Davis," in *The Governors of Arkansas,* pp. 111–125; G. Gregory Kiser, "The Socialist Party in Arkansas, 1900–1912," *Arkansas Historical Quarterly* 40 (Summer 1981): 119–153.

8 Ruined Again

1. Benjamin U. Ratchford, *American State Debts,* pp. 383–405.

2. *Arkansas Gazette,* September 30, 1923; Lew A. Dew, "On a Slow Train Through Arkansas—The Negative Image of Arkansas in the Early Twentieth Century," *Arkansas Historical Quarterly* 39 (Summer 1980): 125–135; Foy Lisenby, "A Survey of Arkansas' Image Problem," *Arkansas Historical Quarterly* 30 (Spring 1971): 60–71.

3. David B. Danbom, *The Resisted Revolution: Urban America and the Industrialization of Agriculture 1900–1930.*

4. Cal Ledbetter, Jr., "The Antievolution Law: Church and State in Arkansas," *Arkansas Historical Quarterly* 38 (Winter 1979): 310–312; the boosters were also ineffective in opposing the Klan, *Arkansas Gazette,* September 11, 1921; Charles C. Alexander, "White Robes in Politics: The Ku Klux Klan in Arkansas, 1922-1924," *Arkansas Historical Quarterly* 22 (Fall 1963): 195–214.

5. *Arkansas Gazette,* October 12, 1925; Winston P. Wilson, *Harvey Couch: The Master Builder.*

6. Charles Orson Cook, "Boosterism and Babbittry: Charles Hillman Brough and the 'Selling' of Arkansas," *Arkansas Historical Quarterly* 36 (Spring 1978): 74–83; *Arkansas Gazette,* October 16, 1921, June 22, 1922, September 30, 1923, November 30, 1924.

7. Robert A. Leflar, "The Bankers' Agricultural Revolt of 1919," *Arkansas Historical Quarterly* 27 (Winter 1968): 273–305; *Arkansas Gazette,* February 1, 1920, January 24, 1926.

8. *Arkansas Gazette,* February 9, 1911, January 19, August 27, 1917; Michael B. Dougan, "The Doctrine of Creative Destruction: Ferry and Bridge Law in Arkansas," *Arkansas Historical Quarterly* 39 (Summer 1980): 151–158.

9. *Arkansas Gazette,* December 5, 1920.

10. Sherman Rogers, "A Defense of Arkansas," *Outlook* 129 (October 26, 1921), pp. 294–298.

11. *New York Times,* March 20–29, 1921.

12. *Arkansas Gazette,* December 22, 1923, December 25, 30, 1926; April 22, 1928; David Y. Thomas ed., *Arkansas and its People* vol. 2, pp. 436–444.

13. *Arkansas Gazette,* September 11, 1926.

14. Ibid., February 6, 1927.

15. Edwin Mims, *The Advancing South* (New York: Doubleday, 1926), pp. vii-xiii, 313.

16. Ratchford, *American State Debts*, pp. 383–387.

17. Ibid., *Arkansas Gazette*, February 26, 1929, January 10, 1932.

18. David Ellery Rison, "Arkansas During the Great Depression," pp. 52–65; Arkansas State Highway Audit Commission Records, 1933–1934, Special Collection, University of Arkansas, Fayetteville; *Arkansas Gazette*, January 11, 1933.

19. Lee Reaves, "Highway Bond Refunding in Arkansas," *Arkansas Historical Quarterly* 2 (December 1943): 316–330.

9 Driving Out the Arkies

1. Leland Duvall, *Arkansas: Colony and State*, p. 23; Gilbert C. Fite, "Southern Agriculture Since the Civil War," *Agricultural History* 53 (January 1979): 3–21.

2. Roger Lambert, "Hoover and the Red Cross in the Arkansas Drought of 1930," *Arkansas Historical Quarterly* 29 (Spring 1970): 3–19; Donald Holley, *Uncle Sam's Farmers: The New Deal Communities in the Lower Mississippi Valley;* David E. Rison, "Arkansas During the Great Depression," pp. 18–26.

3. Tate C. Page, *The Voices of Moccasin Creek*, pp. 411–412.

4. Jerold S. Auerback, "Southern Tenant Farmers: Socialist Critics of the New Deal," *Arkansas Historical Quarterly* 27 (Summer 1968): 113–131; Donald H. Grubbs, *Cry from the Cotton: The Southern Tenant Farmers' Union and the New Deal;* F. Raymond Daniell articles in *Memphis Press-Scimitar,* April 24–30, 1935.

5. Howard Kester, *Revolt Among the Sharecroppers* (New York: Covici, Friede, 1936), pp. 81–85.

6. Holley, *Uncle Sam's Farmers*, pp. 274–283; Jonathan Daniels, *A Southerner Discovers the South* (New York: Macmillan Company, 1938), pp. 138–163.

7. Dolan Burris, *Buttermilk Country* (n.p., n.p., 1980).

8. Donald C. Alexander, *The Arkansas Plantation, 1920–1942;* Oren Stephens, "Revolt on the Delta: What Happened to the Sharecroppers Union," *Harper's* November 1941, pp. 656–664.

9. Bureau of the Census, *Negroes in the United States, 1920–32* (Washington: Government Printing Office, 1935), pp. 36–46.

10. Carey McWilliams, *Ill Fares the Land: Migrants and Migratory Labor in the United States*, pp. 31–35.

11. Piney Page articles in Russellville *Courier-Democrat*, March 16, 1980.

12. Clyde T. Ellis, *A Giant Step* (New York: Random House, 1966), pp. 28–30.

13. Piney Page in Russellville *Courier-Democrat*, September 23, 1979.

14. Gladys K. Bowles, *Farm Population: Net Migration from the Rural Farm—Population 1940–50, Bulletin 176* (Washington: Deparment of Agriculture, 1956); Charles E. Venus, "The Emigration of Arkansas College Graduates," p. 18.

15. "Why do Arkansans Vanish?" *Business Week*, April 12, 1958, pp. 96–97; Phillips H. Brown and John M. Peterson, "The Exodus from Arkansas," *Arkansas Economist*, Winter, 1960, pp. 10–15.

16. Doug Wilson, "Arkansas—No Green Pastures," *Arkansas Traveler,* November 2, 1961, quoted in Venus, "The Emigration of Arkansas College Graduates," p. 9.

17. John Gould Fletcher, *Arkansas*, pp. 400–401.

18. Ibid., pp. 395–396.

19. Haynes Johnson and Bernard M. Gwertzman, *Fulbright: The Dissenter,* p. 74.

10 The Faubus Detour

1. John Gould Fletcher, *Arkansas*, pp. 392–394; O.E. McKnight and Amy Jean Greene, *Living in Arkansas* (Norman: Harlow Publishing, 1963), pp. 315–317; Boyce Drummond, "Arkansas 1940–1954," *Historical Report of the Secretary of the State of Arkansas* vol. 3 (Little Rock, 1978), pp. 175–176.

2. *Business Week*, May 30, 1953, pp. 72–75; *Time*, February 9, 1953, pp. 88–89.

3. Robert A. Leflar, *The First 100 Years: Centennial History of the University of Arkansas*, pp. 91, 97; interview with M.C. Tucker who attended State Teachers.

4. Clyde Brion Davis, "Arkansas," *Holiday*, November 1954, p. 42.

5. Brooks Hays, *Politics is My Parish*, p. 134; Hays, *A Southern Moderate Speaks;* Thomas A. Krueger, *And Promises to Keep* (Nashville: Vanderbilt University Press, 1967), p. 38; Ralph J. Bunche, *The Political Status of the Negro in the Age of F.D.R.* ed. Dewey W. Grantham (Chicago: University of Chicago Press, 1973), pp. 40, 364.

6. Jim Lester, *A Man for Arkansas: Sid McMath and the Southern Reform Tradition*.

7. NPA Committee of the South, *New Industry Comes to the South* (Washington: National Planning Association, 1949) pp. 20–21; Ralph Gray and John B. Webster, "Searcy: A City Reborn," *Arkansas Economist*, Spring 1959, pp. 22–24; James Nathaniel Davis, Jr., "Effects of Industrialization upon the Economy of Searcy, Arkansas."

8. Tom W. Dillard, "Winthrop Rockefeller," in Timothy P. Donovan and Willard B. Gatewood, Jr., eds. *The Governors of Arkansas: Essays in Political Biography,* pp. 226–234; John Ward, *The Arkansas Rockefeller.*

9. David Wallace, "Orval Eugene Faubus" in *The Governors of Arkansas*, p. 220; Wallace, "Orval Faubus: The Central Figure at Little Rock Central High School," *Arkansas Historical Quarterly* 39 (Winter 1980): 314–329.

10. Leflar, *The First 100 Years*, pp. 278–283; Virgil T. Blossom, *It has Happened Here;* Daisy Bates, *The Long Shadow of Little Rock.*

11. The Faubus story can be found in Numan V. Bartley, *The Rise of Massive Resistance* (Baton Rouge: Louisiana State University Press, 1969), pp. 252–264, and Orval Eugene Faubus, *Down From the Hills*, pp. 191–344.

12. Neal R. Peirce, *The Deep South States of America*, p. 132; Robert Sherrill, *Gothic Politics in the Deep South*, p. 89; Wallace, "Orval Faubus: The Central Figure at Little Rock Central High School," pp. 324–328; *Arkansas Gazette*, January 18, 1981.

13. Elizabeth Huckaby, *Crisis at Central High: Little Rock 1957-58*, p. 62.

14. Harry S. Ashmore, *Arkansas: A Bicentennial History*, p. 152; Bruce Catton, "Journalism on Crusade," *Saturday Review*, July 26, 1958, pp. 9–11; Numan V. Bartley and Hugh D. Graham, *Southern Politics and the Second Reconstruction* (Baltimore: Johns Hopkins Press, 1975), pp. 54–55; Ronnie Dugger, "They Like Faubus," *New Republic*, October 14, 1957, pp. 11–13.

15. *Arkansas Gazette*, July 8, 29, 1958.

16. Ibid., July 15, 1958.

17. Bartley, *The Rise of Massive Resistance*, pp.328-331; *Wall Street Journal*, October 1, 1962, December 17, 1963; see also Elizabeth Jacoway, ed., *Southern Businessmen and Desegregation*, pp. 15–41.

18. Wallace, "Orval Eugene Faubus," pp. 222–225; Earl Black, *Southern Governors and Civil Rights* (Cambridge: Harvard University Press, 1976), pp. 98–104.

11 Cinderella Time

1. Dan During, "Arkansas, 1954 to Present" in *Historical Report of the Secretary of State of Arkansas* vol. 3 (Little Rock, 1978), p. 202.

2. Leland Duvall, *Arkansas: Colony and State*, pp. 23–50; S. C. Tucker, Jr., *To Sell A Good Bull: A Story of the Arkansas River Valley*, pp. 158–166.

3. *Arkansas Gazette*, January 24, 1980; Bernard L Weinstein, *Regional Growth and Decline in the United States* (New York: Praeger Publishers, 1978), pp. 134–135, 137.

4. *Directory of Arkansas Manufacturers, 1980* (Little Rock: Arkansas Industrial Dvelopment Commission, 1980), pp. 6–8.

5. Edward M. Penick, "Arkansas and the South," *Arkansas Business and Economic Review*, Winter 1977, pp. 1–8.

6. *Wall Street Journal*, July 29, 1980.

7. Edgar & Patricia Cheatham, "The Arkansas Everybody Knows with a Few New Wrinkles," *Travel*, August 1974, pp. 52–57.

8. Dwight Pitcaithley, "Buffalo River: An Ozark Region from Settlement to National River."

9. Richard E. Yates, "Arkansas: Independent and Unpredictable" in William C. Havard, ed. *The Changing Politics of the South*, p. 241.

10. Timothy P. Donovan and Willard B. Gatewood, Jr., *The Governors of Arkansas: Essays in Political Biography*, pp. 235–248.

11. Ouida O. Clark, "Arkansas Blacks: Progress in 30 Years," *Arkansas Gazette*, July 5, November 26, 1981; Boyd Gibbons, "Easygoing, Hardworking Arkansas," *National Geographic*, March 1979, pp. 396–426.

12. *Arkansas Gazette*, January 5, February 3, 5, 6, 1980.

13. John Gould Fletcher, *Arkansas,* p. 321; E. Glenn Hinson, *A History of Baptists in Arkansas*, pp. 227, 276–280, 353, 358–359, 368, 380.

14. Gene Lyons, "Repealing the Enlightenment," *Harpers*, April 1982, pp. 38–78; *Arkansas Gazette*, December 7–17, 1981, January 10, 1982.

15. Willard B. Gatewood, Jr., "Arkansas: Newest Symbol of the New South" in *The Arkansas Humanities in Perspective*, pp. 18–42.

16. *Arkansas Gazette*, March 6, 1982, January 3, March 12, 1983.

17. For the rankings of Arkansas, see: Charles R. Britton and Thomas O. Graff, "The Role of Older Americans in Arkansas: Changing Population Patterns," *Arkansas Business and Economic Review* 15 (1982): 1–8.

Bibliography

All historians ride on the shoulders of industrious fellow scholars, This is especially true of those who write interpretative surveys for which the sources are too abundant to be read in a single decade. Although I skimmed more than a hundred years of the *Arkansas Gazette,* and even dipped into the manuscripts at the University special collections, this work rests more on the published literature, especially recent articles, dissertations and monographs. Greater quantities of research and writing have been completed in Arkansas during the past generation than in all the previous hundred years. I thank all those who have contributed to writing and publishing this local history.

Books
Alexander, Donald Crichton, *The Arkansas Plantation, 1920–1942.* New Haven: Yale University Press, 1943.
Arkansas Secretary of State. *Historical Report of the Secretary of State of Arkansas,* vol. 3, Little Rock, 1978.
Arsenault, Raymond. *The Wild Ass of the Ozarks: Jeff Davis and the Social Bases of Southern Politics.* Philadephia: Temple University Press, 1984.
Ashmore, Harry S. *Arkansas: A Bicentennial History.* New York: W. W. Norton, 1978.
Bartlett, Richard A. *The New Country; A Social History of the American Frontier, 1776–1890.* New York: Oxford University Press, 1974.
Bass, Jack, and Walter DeVries. *The Transformation of Southern Politics.* New York: Basic Books, 1976.
Bates, Daisy. *The Long Shadow of Little Rock.* New York: David McKay Company, 1962.
Blossom, Virgil T. *It Has Happened Here.* New York: Harper & Brothers, 1959.
Carter, Clarence Edwin. *The Territorial Papers of the United States,* vols. 19, *Arkansas*

1819–1825, and 21, *Arkansas 1829–1836.* Washington: Government Printing Office, 1953 & 1954.

Castel, Albert. *General Sterling Price and the Civil War in the West.* Baton Rouge: Louisiana State University Press, 1968.

Clayton, Powell. *The Aftermath of the Civil War in Arkansas.* New York: Neale Publishing Company, 1915.

Danbom, David B. *The Resisted Revolution: Urban America and the Industrialization of Agriculture, 1900–1930.* Ames: Iowa State University Press, 1979.

Dauberry, Charles Giles Bridle. *Journal of a Tour Through the United States, 1837–38.* Oxford: T. Combe, 1843.

Donaghey, George W. *Building a State Capitol.* Little Rock: Parke-Harper, 1937.

Donovan, Timothy P., and Willard B. Gatewood, Jr., eds., *The Governors of Arkansas: Essays in Political Biography.* Fayetteville: University of Arkansas Press, 1981.

Dougan, Michael B. *Confederate Arkansas: The People and Policies of a Frontier State in Wartime.* University: University of Alabama Press, 1976.

Dunaway, L. S. *Jeff Davis: Governor and United States Senator.* Little Rock: Democrat Printing Co., 1913.

Duvall, Leland. *Arkansas: Colony and State.* Little Rock: Rose Publishing Company, 1969.

Elliott, Charles. *Southwestern Methodism: A History of the M.E. Church from 1844 to 1864.* Cincinnati: Poe & Hitchcock, 1868.

Faubus, Orval Eugene. *Down From the Hills.* Little Rock: Democrat Printing Company, 1980.

Ferguson, John L., and J. H. Atkinson. *Historic Arkansas.* Little Rock: Arkansas History Commission, 1966.

Fletcher, John Gould. *Arkansas.* Chapel Hill: University of North Carolina Press, 1947.

Featherstonhaugh, G. W. *Excursion Through the Slave States,* vol. 2. London: John Murray, 1844.

Flint, Timothy. *Recollections of the Last Ten Years.* Boston: Cummings, Hilliard & Co., 1826.

Gerstacker, Friedrich. *Wild Sports in the Far West: The Narrative of a German Wanderer Beyond the Mississippi, 1837–1843.* Edna L. and Harrison R. Steeves, ed. Durham: Duke University Press, 1968.

Gibbs, Mifflin W. *Shadow and Light: An Autobiography.* New York: Arno Press, 1968.

Gouge, William M., and William R. Miller. *Report of the Accountants Appointed Under the Act of January 15, 1855, to Investigate the Affairs of the Real Estate Bank of Arkansas.* Little Rock: True Democrat Office, 1856.

Grubbs, Donald H. *Cry From the Cotton: The Southern Tenant Farmers' Union and the New Deal.* Chapel Hill: University of North Carolina Press, 1971.

Hallum, John. *Biographical and Pictorial History of Arkansas.* Albany: Weed, Parsons & Co., 1887.

Harrell, John M. *Arkansas.* vol. 10 of Clement A. Evans, *Confederate Military History.* Atlanta: Confederate Publishing Co., 1899.

_____. *The Brooks and Baxter War: A History of the Reconstruction Period in Arkansas.* St. Louis: Slawson Printing Co., 1893.

Harrington, Fred Harvey. *Hanging Judge.* Caldwell: Caxton Printers, 1951.

Hays, Brooks. *Politics is My Parish.* Baton Rouge: Louisiana State University Press, 1981.

_____. *A Southern Moderate Speaks*. Chapel Hill: University of North Carolina Press, 1959.

Herndon, Dallas T. *Centennial History of Arkansas*. 3 vols. Chicago: S. J. Clarke Publishing Co., 1922.

Hinson, E. Glenn. *A History of Baptists in Arkansas, 1818–1978*. Little Rock: Arkansas Baptist State Convention, 1979.

Holley, Donald. *Uncle Sam's Farmers: The New Deal Communities in the Lower Mississippi Valley*. Urbana: University of Illinois Press, 1975.

Huckaby, Elizabeth. *Crisis at Central High: Little Rock, 1957–58*. Baton Rouge: Louisiana State University Press, 1980.

Jacobson, Charles. *The Life Story of Jeff Davis: The Stormy Petrel of Arkansas Politics*. Little Rock: Parke-Harper Publishing Co., 1925.

Jacoway, Elizabeth, ed. *Southern Businessmen and Desegregation*. Baton Rouge: Louisiana State University Press, 1982.

Johnson, Haynes, and Bernard M. Gwertzman. *Fulbright; The Dissenter*. Garden City: Doubleday & Company, 1968.

Kousser, J. Morgan. *The Shaping of Southern Politics: Suffrage Restriction and the Establishment of the One-Party South, 1880–1910*. New Haven: Yale University Press, 1974.

Leflar, Robert A. *The First 100 Years: Centennial History of the University of Arkansas*. Fayetteville: University of Arkansas Foundation, 1972.

Lester, Jim. *A Man for Arkansas: Sid McMath and the Southern Reform Tradition*. Little Rock: Rose Publishing Company, 1976.

Leyburn, James G. *The Scotch-Irish: A Social History*. Chapel Hill: University of North Carolina Press, 1962.

Lillard, Richard G. *The Great Forest*. New York: Alfred A. Knopf, 1947.

McCool, B. Boren. *Union, Reaction and Riot: Biography of a Rural Race Riot*. Memphis: Bureau of Social Research, 1970.

McGrane, Reginald C. *Foreign Bondholders and American State Debts*. New York: Macmillan Company, 1935.

McMillen, Neil R. *The Citizens' Council: Organized Resistance to the Second Reconstruction, 1954–64*. Urbana: University of Illinois Press, 1971.

McWilliams, Carey. *Ill Fares the Land: Migrants and Migratory Labor in the United States*. Boston: Little, Brown, 1942.

Mathews, Donald G. *Religion in the Old South*. Chicago: University of Chicago Press, 1977.

Monks, William. *A History of Southern Missouri and Northern Arkansas*. West Plains: West Plains Journal Co., 1907.

Morgan, W. Scott. *History of the Wheeel and Alliance and the Impending Revolution*. St. Louis: Woodward, 1891.

Nash, Charles Edward. *Biographical Sketches of Gen. Pat Cleburne and Gen. T. C. Hindman*. Little Rock: Tunnah & Pittard, 1898.

Noland, Charles F. M. *Pete Whetstone of Devil's Fork*. ed. Ted R. Worley and Eugene A. Nolte. VanBuren: Press-Argus, 1957.

Nordhoff, Charles. *The Cotton States in the Spring and Summer of 1875*. New York: Burt Franklin, 1876.

Nuttall, Thomas. *Journal of Travels into the Arkansas Territory During the Year 1819*. ed. Reuben Gold Thwaites. Cleveland: Arthur H. Clark Co., 1905.

Page, Tate C. *The Voices of Moccasin Creek*. Point Lookout: School of the Ozarks Press, 1972.

Peirce, Neal R. *The Deep South States of America*. New York: W. W. Norton, 1974.

Pickens, William. *Bursting Bonds*. Boston: Jordan and More, 1923.

Pope, William F. *Early Days in Arkansas*. Little Rock: Frederick W. Allsopp, 1895.

Ratchford, Benjamin U. *American State Debts*. Durham: Duke University Press, 1941.

Rawick, George P. *The American Slave: A Composite Autbiography*, vols. 8–11. Westport: Greenwood Publishing Co., 1972.

Rogers, J. S. *History of Arkansas Baptists*. Little Rock: Arkansas Baptist State Convention, 1948.

Rohrbough, Malcolm J. *The Trans-Appalachian Frontier*. New York: Oxford University Press, 1978.

Ross, Margaret Smith. *Arkansas Gazette: The Early Years, 1819–66*. Little Rock: Arkansas Gazette Foundation, 1969.

Rudd, Dan A., and Theo. Bond. *From Slavery to Wealth: The Life of Scott Bond*. Madison: The Journal Printing Co., 1917.

Schoolcraft, Henry R. *A View of the Lead Mines of Missouri*. New York: Charles Wiley & Co., 1819.

Sharp, James Roger. *The Jacksonians versus the Banks: Politics in the States after the Panic of 1837*. New York Columbia University Press, 1970.

Sherrill, Robert. *Gothic Politics in the Deep South*. New York: Grossman Publishers, 1968.

Shinn, Josiah H. *Pioneers and Makers of Arkansas*. Little Rock: Genealogical and Historical Publishing Company, 1908.

Shirley, Glenn. *Law West of Fort Smith*. Lincoln; University of Nebraska Press, 1968.

Smith, John I. *The Courage of a Southern Unionist: A Biography of Isaac Murphy*. Little Rock: Rose Publishing Co., 1979

Staples, Thomas S. *Reconstruction in Arkansas 1862–1874* New York: Columbia University Press, 1923.

Stinnett, T. M., and Clara B. Kennan. *All This and Tomorrow Too*. Little Rock: Arkansas Education Association, 1969.

Taylor, Orville W. *Negro Slavery in Arkansas*. Durham: Duke University Press, 1958.

Thomas, David Y. *Arkansas and its People: A History, 1541–1930*. 2 vols. New York: American Historical Society, 1930.

_____. *Arkansas in War and Reconstruction, 1861–1874*. Little Rock: United Daughters of the Confederacy, 1926.

Thompson, George H. *Arkansas and Reconstruction: The Influence of Geography, Economics and Personality*. Port Washington: Kennikat Press, 1976.

Trelease, Allen W. *White Terror: The Ku Klux Klan Conspiracy and Southern Reconstruction*. New York: Harper & Row, 1971.

Tucker, S. C., Jr. *To Sell a Good Bull: A Story of the Arkansas River Valley*. Danville: Danville Bicentennial History, 1976.

Vernon, Walter N. *Methodism in Arkansas, 1816–1976*. Little Rock: Joint Committee for the History of Arkansas Methodism, 1976.

_____. *William Stevenson: Riding Preacher*. Dallas: Southern Methodist University Press, 1964.

Ward, John L. *The Arkansas Rockefeller*. Baton Rouge: Louisiana State University Press, 1978.

White, Lonnie J. *Politics on the Southwestern Frontier: Arkansas Territory, 1819–1836.* Memphis: Memphis State University Press, 1964.

Wilson, Winston P. *Harvey Couch: The Master Builder.* Nashville: Broadman's Press, 1947.

Wolf, John Quincy, Jr., ed. *Life in the Leatherwoods.* Memphis, Memphis State University Press, 1974.

Woodward, C. Vann. *Origins of the New South.* Baton Rouge: Louisiana State University Press, 1951.

Worthen, W. B. *Early Banking in Arkansas.* Little Rock: Democrat Printing Co., 1906.

WPA Writers Program. *Arkansas: A Guide to the State.* New York: Hastings House, 1941.

Dissertations

Arsenault, Raymond O. "The Wild Ass of the Ozarks: Jeff Davis and the Social Bases of Southern Demagoguery, 1888–1913" (Ph.D. dissertation, Brandeis University, 1981).

Bayliss, Garland Erastus. "Public Affairs in Arkansas 1874–1896" (Ph.D. dissertation, University of Texas, 1972).

Boyett, Gene Wells. "The Whigs of Arkansas, 1836–1856" (Ph.D. dissertation, Louisiana State University, 1972).

Carmichael, Maude. "The Plantation System in Arkansas, 1850–1876" (Ph.D. dissertation, Radcliffe, 1935).

Cook, Charles O. "Arkansas's Charles Hillman Brough, 1876–1935: An Interpretation" (Ph.D. dissertation, University of Houston, 1980).

Davis, James N. "Effects of Industrialization Upon the Economy of Searcy, Arkansas" (Ph.D. dissertation, University of Arkansas, 1963).

Ellenburg, Martha Ann. "Reconstruction in Arkansas" (Ph.D. dissertation, University of Missouri, 1967).

Ferguson, John. "William E. Woodruff and the Territory of Arkansas, 1819–1836" (Ph.D. dissertation, Tulane, 1960).

Graves, John William. "Town and Country: Race Relations and Urban Development in Arkansas, 1865–1905" (Ph.D. dissertation, University of Virginia, 1978).

Moore, Waddy William. "Territorial Arkansas, 1819–1836" (Ph.D. dissertation, University of North Carolina, 1963).

Neal, Nevin Emil. "A Biography of Joseph T. Robinson," (Ph.D. dissertation, University of Oklahoma, 1958).

Niswonger, Richard Leverne. "Arkansas Democratic Politics, 1896–1920" (Ph.D. dissertation, University of Texas, 1974).

Pitcaithley, Dwight Towsend. "Buffalo River: An Ozark Region From Settlement to National River" (Ph.D. dissertation, Texas Tech, 1976).

Rison, David Ellery. "Arkansas During the Great Depression" (Ph.D. dissertation, University of California-Los Angeles, 1974).

Segraves, Joe Tolbert. "Arkansas Politics, 1874–1918" (Ph.D. dissertation, University of Kentucky, 1973).

Smith, C. Calvin. "Arkansas, 1940–45: Public and Press Reaction to War and Wartime Pressures" (Ph.D. dissertation, University of Arkansas. 1978).

Stokes, Dewey Allen, Jr. "Public Affairs in Arkansas, 1836–1850" (Ph.D. dissertation, University of Texas, 1966).

Venus, Charles E. "The Emigration of Arkansas College Graduates" (Ph.D. dissertation, University of Arkansas, 1964).

Walz, Robert Bradshaw. "Migration Into Arkansas, 1834–1880" (Ph.D. dissertation, University of Texas, 1958).

Wheeler, John McDaniel. "The People's Party in Arkansas, 1891–1896" (Ph.D. dissertation, Tulane University, 1975).

Articles

Good articles are too abundant for listing but most may be located by consulting Walter R. Brown's *Arkansas Historical Quarterly Index* (Fayetteville: Arkansas Historical Association, 1981). Other especially important articles are: Willard B. Gatewood, Jr., "Arkansas: Newest Symbol of the New South" in *The Arkansas Humanities in Perspective* (Magnolia: Southern Arkansas University, 1979), pp. 18–42; Stephen F. Strausberg, "The Effectiveness of the New Deal in Arkansas," in Donald W. Whisenhunt, ed. *The Depression in the Southwest* (Port Washington N.Y.: Kennikat Press, 1980), pp. 102–116; Richard E. Yates, "Arkansas: Independent and Unpredictable," in William C. Havard, ed., *The Changing Politics of the South.* (Baton Rouge: Louisiana State University Press, 1972), and O. W. Taylor, "Revival and Growth of Organized Religion in Arkansas after the Civil War" in Samuel S. Hill, ed., *Religion in the Southern States* (Macon, Ga.: Mercer University Press, 1983).

Index